# FEMALE WARRIORS: MEMORIALS OF FEMALE VALOUR AND HEROISM, FROM THE MYTHOLOGICAL AGES TO THE PRESENT ERA, VOL. I

Published @ 2017 Trieste Publishing Pty Ltd

ISBN 9780649582280

Female Warriors: Memorials of Female Valour and Heroism, from the Mythological Ages to the Present Era, Vol. I by Eleanor C. Clayton

Edited by Trieste Publishing Pty Ltd.
 Cover @ 2017

www.triestepublishing.com

# ELEANOR C. CLAYTON

# FEMALE WARRIORS: MEMORIALS OF FEMALE VALOUR AND HEROISM, FROM THE MYTHOLOGICAL AGES TO THE PRESENT ERA, VOL. I

Trieste

# FEMALE WARRIORS.

# FEMALE WARRIORS.

### MEMORIALS OF

## *FEMALE VALOUR AND HEROISM, FROM*

## *THE MYTHOLOGICAL AGES TO THE PRESENT ERA.*

BY

## ELLEN C. CLAYTON

### (*MRS. NEEDHAM*),

AUTHOR OF

### "QUEENS OF SONG," "ENGLISH FEMALE ARTISTS," Etc.

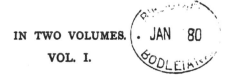

IN TWO VOLUMES.

VOL. I.

### LONDON:

## TINSLEY BROTHERS, 8, CATHERINE STREET, STRAND.

### 1879.

PRINTED BY TAYLOR AND CO.,
10, LITTLE QUEEN STREET, LINCOLN'S INN FIELDS.

THIS SHORT RECORD IS

𝕯𝖊𝖉𝖎𝖈𝖆𝖙𝖊𝖉,

IN TOKEN OF AFFECTION AND ESTEEM,

TO

MADAME RONNIGER.

# CONTENTS.

———◆———

# LIST OF THE

# PRINCIPAL AUTHORITIES CONSULTED.

———————◆———————

Beloe's Herodotus.

Booth's Diodorus Siculus.

Hearne's Justin.

Murphy's Tacitus.

Suetonius (Bohn's Classical Library).

Abbé Guyon.   Histoire des Amazones.   Paris, 1740.

Rollin.   Histoire Ancienne.

Grote.   History of Greece.

Gibbon.   Decline and Fall of the Roman Empire.

Mills.   History of Mohammedism.

Neale.   Islamism : its Rise and Progress.

Miss Strickland.   Queens of England and Scotland.

Mrs. Matthew Hall.   Queens of England before the Conquest.

Mrs. Forbes Bush.   Queens of France.

Michaud.   Histoire des Croisades.

Lingard.   History of England.

Sir J. Mackintosh.   History of England.

Tytler.   History of Scotland ; and Worthies of Scotland.

Wolfgang Menzel.   History of Germany (Mrs. Geo. Horrocks).

Kelly.   History of Russia.

Coxe.   House of Austria.

Motley.   Rise of the Dutch Republic.

Berriat St. Prix.   Jeanne d'Arc.   Paris, 1817.

Lebrun des Charmettes.   Hist. de Jeanne d'Arc.   Paris, 1817.

Jollois.   Hist. Abrégée de la Vie et Exploits de Jeanne d'Arc.   Paris, 1821.

Prescott.   Conquest of Mexico.

Ralegh's Guiana.   With Introduction and Notes, by Sir Robert Schomburgh (Hackluyt Society).

Life of Mrs. Christian Davies, *alias* Mother Ross.   London, 1741 (Defoe).

Lamartine.   Hist of theGirondists.   (Capt. Rafter)

Sir John Carr.   Tour through Spain.

Maria Graham.   Journal of a Voyage to Brazil, etc.

Garibaldi. An Autobiography. Edited by Alexandre Dumas.

Scenes of the Civil War in Hungary, with the Personal Adventures of an Austrian Officer. London, 1850.

Ferishta. History of Mahommedan India (Jo. Briggs). 1828.

Ferishta. History of the Dekkan, and History of Bengal (J. Scott). 1794.

Gladwin. History of Hindostan.

Francklin. History of Shah Aulum, Emperor of Hindostan.

Private Life of an Eastern King.

Nolan. Illustrated History of British India.

Bruce's Travels.

Winwood Reade  SavageAfri ca.  1864.

Duncan. Travels in Dahomey. 1847.

Captain Burton. Mission to Dahomé. 1864.

Matilda Betham. Cyclopædia of Female Biography.

Mrs. Ellet. Women Artists.

Fullom. History of Woman.

Mrs. Hale. Woman's Record.

Mrs. Starling. Noble Deeds of Woman.

Watson. Heroic Women of History. Philadelphia. 1852.

Wilson's Wonderful Characters. 1821.

Kirby's Wonderful and Eccentric Museum. 1820.
Annual Register.
Notes and Queries.
Illustrated London News. Galignani.
Edinburgh Annual Register.
Biographie Universelle.
Ec. etc.

# FEMALE WARRIORS.

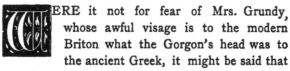

I.

Mythology. — Warlike Goddesses. — The Amazons. — The Sarmatians.—The Machlyes and Auses.—The Zaveces.— More Modern Tribes of Amazons in Asia and Africa.

ERE it not for fear of Mrs. Grundy, whose awful visage is to the modern Briton what the Gorgon's head was to the ancient Greek, it might be said that Popular Prejudice is the deaf, deformed sister of Justice. Popular Prejudice makes up her mind on certain subjects, and is grandly unconscious of any fault within herself; ignorant that she · is deaf, and that she is morally blind, although able to see every petty object that passes within her range. Popular Prejudice, like her stately cousin, Mrs. Grundy, arranges fixed rules of etiquette, of conduct, even of feeling, and never pardons the slightest infringement of the lines she marks out. A man may lay down his life for "an idea," but if it be outside the ramparts of Popular Prejudice, he does so as a rebel, maybe a fool. A man may have high aspirations, but if by the breadth of a hair's line they run not parallel with the views of Popular Prejudice, let him be anathema maranatha, let him be bound in chains, away with him to outer darkness, to the company of the few who share his—"crotchets."

Whisper it not in Gath that a woman should dare ever to transgress the lines laid down by Popular Prejudice. A woman is a subordinate accident in Creation, quite an afterthought, a supplementary notion, a postscript, though Humour might laughingly say, much like the famous postscript to a lady's letter. Man (though he is permitted to include in his superb all-comprehensive identity, Woman) is big, strong, noble, intellectual : a Being. Woman is small, weak, seldom noble, and ought not to be conscious of the significance of the word Intellectual.

The exception is supposed to prove the rule. A woman may be forgiven for defying Popular Prejudice, if she is very pretty, very silly, and very wicked. Popular Prejudice has the natural instinct of yielding to any little weakness that may be imagined to flatter a Man. But Popular Prejudice

is superbly angry with a woman who is perhaps not
pretty, yet ventures to claim good sense and personal
will, and who may be innately good.  Popular Prejudice is the fast friend of lean-faced Envy ; and woe
betide the woman (or even the man) who would
presume to sit down at the board of these allies
uninvited.

Popular Prejudice, having decided that woman is a
poor, weak creature, credulous, easily influenced,
holds that she is of necessity timid ; that if she were
allowed as much as a voice in the government of her
native country, she would stand appalled if war were
even hinted at.  If it be proved by hard facts that
woman is not a poor, weak creature, then she must
be reprimanded as being masculine.  To brand a
woman as being masculine, is supposed to be quite
sufficient to drive her cowering back to her 'broidery-
frame and her lute.

Popular Prejudice abhors hard facts, and rarely
reads history.  Yet nobody can deny that facts are
stubborn things, or that the world rolls calmly round
even when wars, rumours of wars, revolutions, and
counter-revolutions, are raging in every quarter and
sub-division of its surface.

War is, undoubtedly, a horrid alternative to the
average woman, and she shrinks from it—as the
average man shrinks.  But, walking down the serried
ranks of history, we find strange records of feminine

bravery; as we might discover singular instances of masculine cowardice, if we searched far enough.

As argumentation is unpleasant and unprofitable, be it counted only idle pastime gathering a handful of memories from the playground of history.

Opinion among the ancients on all subjects was as fairly divided as it has been among moderns. Naturally, however, in that uncivilised stage of the world's development, men and women inclined more towards brute force than they now do. Plato, the Athenian philosopher, lamented that the lives of women should be wasted in domestic, and sometimes servile, duties; arguing that if the girls were trained like the boys, in athletic sports and warlike exercises, and were taught to endure fatigue, they would soon cease to be the weaker sex, and could not only fight as well as their lords and masters, but might take the command of armies and fleets.

But though the counsels of the great Athenian were followed in many things, they were entirely declined on this question. His countrymen, even in cases of the direst necessity, were loth to swell their ranks with female recruits; and it was only during the degenerate days of the Empire that Rome publicly authorised the combats of women in the amphitheatre.

Very few people deny that woman did, occasionally, fight in olden times. All nations, from the rudest barbarians to those most advanced in civilisation, hold this belief. An old Chinese tradition says that but for the wisdom of certain mandarins in days gone by, the weaker sex might possibly be now the stronger in the Celestial Empire. Once upon a time, so the story runs, the Chinese women, discontented with the unequal share accorded to them in the government, rose in rebellion. The revolt so very nearly became a revolution that the Emperor and his ministers, to prevent a recurrence of the danger, decreed that henceforth the feet of girls throughout China should be bandaged in such a way as to put it out of their power ever again to take the field as warriors. And thus, says the fable, originated the famous Golden Lilies.

The ancients were all familiar with the idea of women sometimes exchanging the spindle and distaff for the spear and shield. Not only did they believe their goddesses to take part occasionally in the battles of mortals, but the supreme direction of military affairs was assigned to a female, as Goddess of War; and this deity, combining wisdom and courage, frequently proved more than a match for the brutal if not blundering God of Battles. " Which, indeed," observes Pope, " is no more than just, since wisdom is generally averse to entering into warlike contests at all ; yet when engaged, it is likely to triumph over brute force, and to bear off the laurels of the day." No general amongst the ancients would have dared to enter an enemy's country, besiege a city, or risk an engagement without first sacrificing to the Goddess of War.

All nations alike held the same belief. The Egyptians offered sacrifices to Neith, the Goddess of War, Philosophy, and Wisdom, to whom lions were subject, and whose fitting emblem was the vulture. The Greeks and Romans adored Minerva, the Thunderer's armour-clad daughter : and Bellona, sister, or perhaps wife of Mars, whose chariot she was said to drive through the din and tumult of the fight, lashing the foaming horses with a bloody scourge. And Victoria, whose name denotes her office, was so greatly honoured both in Greece and Rome, that Hiero, King of Syracuse, to flatter the Romans, once sent them an idol figure of this goddess, three hundred and twenty pounds in weight, made of solid gold ; while the Egyptians, who worshipped her under the name of Naphte, represented her in the form of an eagle, because that bird is the strongest of aerial warriors, and invariably victorious over all the feathered race. The Brahmins, who claim an antiquity as great as, or greater than, Egypt, worshipped, and still worship, Durga, or Katyayini, whose ten arms and hands, each of which grasps a warlike weapon or emblem, prove how formidable a foe she is believed to have been. Our ancient British forefathers prayed

to Andate, or Andraste, Goddess of Victory, and called
upon her in their hour of need.   The northern races,
Goths, Vandals, Germans, who over-ran Europe
during the decline of the Roman Empire, assigned a
somewhat analogous place in their mythology to the
Valkyrias, or Disas—

> " Those dread maids, whose hideous yell
> Maddens the battle's bloody swell."

These beautiful women were believed to take a leading part in every battle fought on earth.   Mounted
on swift steeds, armed with helmets and mail, drawn
swords in their hands, they rode wildly over the
field to select those heroes destined by Odin for the
slaughter, and lead them to Valhalla, the Paradise
of the Brave.

Nor is the belief in warlike goddesses confined to
the Old World.   When Cortez entered Mexico, he
found the subjects of Montezuma worshipping,
amongst other deities, all more or less repulsive to
the eye, a horrid basalt monster named Teoyamiqui,
Goddess of War.   She was supposed to be wife of
the equally terrible Huitzilopochtli, or Tlacahuepan-
cuexcotzin, the Mexican Mars.   Like the Valkyrias,
her chief duty was to conduct those warriors who
fell in defence of the gods to the house of the Sun, the
Elysium or Valhalla of the Mexicans, where she
transformed them into humming-birds.

The present age is a decidedly sceptical one.

It is the fashion nowadays to sneer at the traditions venerated by our grandfathers. Those chapters in the world's history which have not been *proved* by *facts*, have passed, in the opinion of many well educated people, into the category of fable and nursery-rhyme. The early histories of Greece and Rome, and of our own country too, are now taken, if taken at all, *cum grano salis*. King Arthur, Hengist and Horsa, and many another hero of whom we were once so proud, have been cast, by most matter-of-fact writers, on the same dusty shelf with Achilles and Hector, Romulus and Remus, side by side with Jupiter and Mercury, Jack the Giant-Killer and Blue Beard. Scarcely anybody in our days is so credulous as to believe that the Amazons ever existed. "Amongst barbarous nations," observes Gibbon, "women have often combated by the side of their husbands; but it is *almost* impossible that a society of Amazons could have existed in the old or new world." His opinion has been endorsed by most subsequent writers, some of whom are even more positive in their expressions of incredulity.

Ancient writers are divided on the question. Strabo denies that there ever was or could have been such a community, and adds, to believe in their existence we must suppose "in those days

the women were men and the men women."
Plutarch, more moderate, half believes they did
exist, but doubts most of their marvellous achievements, which, he thinks, "clearly resemble fable
and fiction." Amongst those who speak for the
defence, Herodotus, Diodorus Siculus, Justin, and
Quintus Curtius stand prominently forward.

Their origin, as related by Justin, though curious,
is far from being impossible or even improbable in
the remote days when they lived. Some years
previous to the reign of Ninus, king of Assyria, two
young princes of the Scythian blood-royal, Hylinos
and Scolopitos, being driven from their native
country by a faction of the nobility, induced several
hundred young men and women to emigrate with
them. After a toilsome march through barren
wilds they settled at last in Cappadocia, on the
rugged banks of the Thermodon. This little river,
which now bears the name of Termeh or Karmili,
falls into the Black Sea, between Trebisond and
Sinope.

For a number of years, the new-comers carried on
a species of border warfare with the natives of the
Themiscyrean plains—stealing their cattle, tearing
up their corn, destroying their homes by fire and
sword. At last the aborigines surprised and massacred
the male settlers, by means of an ambush. The
wives of the latter, having now no one to whom they

could look for protection, armed themselves and expelled the foe from their territory.

From this time they laid aside all thoughts of marriage, "calling it slavery and not matrimony." And, to enforce this law, it is said, they murdered a few men who had escaped the fury of the natives in the general massacre. The Amazons were thenceforth forbidden even to speak to men, save during certain days in the year. At the appointed time, throwing aside their military character, they visited the surrounding nations, and were permitted, by special treaties, to depart again unmolested. Justin says they strangled all their male children directly they were born; Diodorus, that they distorted their limbs; while Philastratus and others affirm that they sent them back, uninjured, to the fathers.

The girls were bred, like their mothers, "not in idleness, nor spinning, but in exercises of war, such as hunting and riding." In early childhood the right breast was burnt off, that they might, when grown up, be more easily able to bend the bow and hurl the dart. From whence, some say, they derived the name of Amazon, which is formed of two Greek words, signifying "wanting a breast." Bryant, the antiquarian, rejects this theory, and suggests, though with less probability, that the name comes from *Zon*, the Sun, which was the national object of worship.

The bow was their favourite weapon, and from
constant practice they acquired such proficiency as
to equal, if not surpass the Scythians and Parthians,
who were the most skilful archers of ancient times.
With the Greeks and Romans it was not uncommon
to speak of a very superior bow or quiver as
" Amazonian."

The nation soon became formidable, and in due
time grew famous throughout the world. At one
time the dominion of the Amazons extended over the
entire of Asia Minor and Ionia, besides a great part
of Italy. So renowned did they at last become, that
Jobates, king of Lycia, commanded Bellerophon to
effect their subjugation, feeling certain that the hero
would never return ; great indeed was his astonishment to see the redoubtable conqueror of the Chimera
return victorious, and he no longer hesitated to
confess the divine origin of the hero. It is said that
Cadmus, the founder of Thebes, was married to an
Amazon named Sphynx when he carried letters from
Egypt to Greece, about 1550 B.C.

Lampedo and Marpesia were the first Amazon
queens whose names became known beyond their
own dominions. To give greater *éclat* to their numerous victories, they claimed to be daughters of the
God Mars—a common expedient in the olden times.
Taking it in turn to defend the frontier and invade
foreign countries, they speedily conquered Iberia

(Georgia), Colchis (Mingrelia), Albania, the Tauric
Chersonese (the Crimea), and a great part of Asia.

To commemorate the achievements of Queen Marpesia during her passage over the craggy and snow-
capped Caucasus, when every peak, every ridge was
bravely defended by hordes of desperate mountaineers,
the name of Mount Marpesia was bestowed upon one
of the loftiest rocks.

It was Marpesia who founded Themiscyra, the
capital of the Amazons, on the banks of the Thermodon. She adorned this city with many stately
buildings, conspicuous amongst which was the royal
palace. Many cities in Asia Minor owed their origin
to the same queen—amongst others, Ephesus,
Thyatira, Smyrna, and Magnesia.

On the death of Marpesia, who was surrounded
by the barbarians during an expedition into Asia, and,
together with her entire army, put to the sword, Orithya, Orseria, or Sinope, and her sister Antiope, or Hippolyte, ascended the throne. Orithya, the most
famous of all the Amazon queens, inherited the
beauty, together with the military skill of her mother,
Marpesia. Under her rule the nation became so
renowned, that Eurystheus, fancying he had at last
found a task beyond the powers of Hercules, commanded the hero, as his ninth labour, to bring him
the girdle of the Amazon queen. The hero succeeded,
however.

Hercules, accompanied by Theseus, Castor and Pollux, and most of the young princes of Greece, sailed to the Euxine with a fleet of nine ships, landed at the mouth of the Thermodon, during the temporary absence of Orithya with the best part of the army, and gained an easy victory over Antiope, whose sister Menalippe he made prisoner; restoring her to liberty in exchange for a suit of the royal armour, including, of course, the girdle.

Historians differ as to the expedition of Theseus. Some say he took away Hippolyte or Antiope, at the same time that Hercules captured her sister; others, however, relate that he undertook a separate vogage many years after that of Hercules, and carried Antiope to Greece, where he made her his queen. Plutarch, in his life of Theseus, gives many details of this latter expedition.

When Orithya heard of the invasion, and of the part which the Athenian prince had acted in it, she vowed not to rest till she was revenged. Calling her subjects together, she soon found herself at the head of many thousand warriors. At her entreaty, Sagillus, king of Scythia, furnished a squadron of horse, commanded by his nephew, Panasagorus. Passing through Colchis, over Mount Caucasus, and crossing an arm of the Cimmerian Bosphorus, which, tradition says, was frozen, the Amazons marched victoriously through Taurica, Thrace, Thessaly, Macedonia,

Attica, and entered the city of Athens. A hard-
fought battle in the streets—described in detail by
old Plutarch—ended by the total rout of the Amazons,
who were compelled to take refuge in the camp of
the Scythians—the latter, in consequence of a quarrel,
having taken no part in the engagement.

The fate of Orithya is unknown, and historians
differ as to that of Antiope. Some say she fell in
the battle by the hand of an Amazon, while fighting
in the Athenian ranks, side by side with Theseus;
but according to others, it was her mediation which
brought about a treaty of peace some four months
later.

Theseus and the Amazon queen had a son named
Hippolytus, or Demophoon, who afterwards ascended
the throne of Athens.

That the Amazons survived this defeat is evident,
since, years after this, we find the Phrygians imploring
aid of Priam, king of Troy, against Myrene, queen
of the Amazons. Little is known about this war,
save that the queen lost her life, and was succeeded
by the beautiful Penthesilea, who not only made
peace with Priam, but led a chosen band of Amazons
to the assistance of Troy when it was besieged by
the Greeks. She arrived shortly after the death of
Hector, and, some declare, seemed, in the eyes of
the old king, destined to take the place of the deceased hero. New life was infused into the dejected

Trojans. But, alas! their joy was short-lived. The morning after her arrival Penthesilea fell by the hand of the invincible Achilles, who, struck by her exquisite beauty, repented too late of what he had done. The sarcastic Thersites jeered and derided, as usual, till the hero, in a fury, turned on the sneering old wretch and slew him. Diomedes, enraged at the death of his mocking old comrade, dragged the corpse of the Amazon queen from the camp, and flung it into the Scamander.

Pliny ascribes the invention of the battle-axe to this queen.

After the death of Penthesilea we learn nothing of the Amazons until the days of Alexander the Great. When that conqueror arrived at Zadracarta, the capital of Hyrcania, about the year B.C. 330, he is said to have been visited by an Amazon queen named Minithya, or Thalestris, who—like another Queen of Sheba—having heard of his mighty achievements, travelled through many lands to see him, followed by an army of female warriors. After staying thirteen days she returned home, greatly disappointed with the personal appearance of the Macedonian king, who, contrary to her expectations, proved, 'tis said, to be a little man.

This is the last we ever hear of the great female nation. Some Roman authors affirm that the Amazons, in alliance with the Albanians, fought

most valiantly in a battle against Pompey the
Great, B.C. 66. But the only ground for this
assertion consisted in the fact that some painted
shields and buskins were found on the battle-field.

If we may believe Herodotus, the Sauromatæ,
or Sarmatians, in Scythia, were descended from
the Amazons. This historian relates how, after a
victory gained by the Greeks over the Amazons near
the Thermodon, the victors distributed their prisoners
into three ships, and set sail for Greece. Once
upon the open sea, the captives rose upon their
guards and put them to death. Being totally
ignorant of navigation and the management of sails,
oars, or rudder, they resigned themselves to the
mercy of winds and waves. They were carried to
the Palus Mæotis (the Sea of Azof), where the
liberated Amazons resumed their arms, sprang on
shore, and meeting a stud of horses, mounted them,
and commenced plundering the natives.

The people, ignorant alike of the dress, the
language, or the country of the invaders, supposed
them to be a body of young men. A sanguinary
battle, however, led to mutual explanations. The
Amazons consented to accept an equal number of
young Scythians as husbands; but afraid that their
habits would never assimilate with those of the
mothers and sisters of their husbands,—for the
Scythian women, so far from going to battle, passed

their days in the wagons—resolved to seek out some desert land where they would be free to follow their own manners and customs. Crossing the Tanais (the Don), they travelled six days' journey east and north, and set up their homes in an un-inhabited country. The nation increased greatly in the course of two or three centuries, and, even in the days of Herodotus, retained the habits of their progenitors. The women pursued the chase on horseback, sometimes with, sometimes without their husbands, and, dressed like men, they fought in battle.

No maiden was permitted to marry till she had first killed an enemy; " it sometimes, therefore, happens," quaintly adds the historian, " that many women die single at an advanced age." Hippocrates says they were condemned to single-blessedness till they had slain at least *three* enemies.

Yet, in spite of this, there was only one Sarmatian queen who became famous for her deeds on the battle-field. This was Amagia, whose husband, King Medosac, having given himself up to indolence and luxury, permitted the affairs of the nation to fall into disorder. At last Amagia took the reins of government into her own hands, received ambas-sadors, took the command of the army, went in person to reinforce the frontiers with troops, and not only repelled several invasions but even made

some incursions into foreign countries to assist such
of her allies as were in peril. Very soon she
became an important personage, and was more
than once chosen as mediatrix by the various petty
monarchs of the Chersonese.

As a ruler, Queen Amagia had not her equal in
those days throughout Scythia. Her judgments
were sound; and both as a general and as a
governor, she was respected by all. Her justice
was severe and unbending, and untempered with
mercy.

The African Amazons, who are said to have
existed for some centuries prior to those of
Thermodon, were not, like the latter, a community
of women only, but the men were kept in close
subjection to their better-halves, by whom they were
treated as women are usually treated in barbarous
countries. While the women conducted the government or fought with their neighbours, the men
staid at home, attending to the household duties.
They were not permitted, under any circumstances,
to serve as soldiers or hold any public office. The
girls were not allowed to marry till they had served
a certain number of years in the army; and, like
the Asiatic Amazons, one breast was burnt off.

This nation, Diodorus tells us, originally dwelt on
a large island called Hesperia, on the western coast

of Africa. This isle, which, the historian says, abounded "with all sorts of fruit trees," is supposed to have been one of the Canaries. The climate was then, as now, delicious, the soil more than ordinarily fertile, and the natives possessed "many herds of cattle and flocks of sheep and goats."

The Amazons, more warlike than their neighbours, speedily conquered the entire island; and, crossing into Africa, subdued great part of Numidia and founded a large city named Chersonesus, in the Tritonis Morass. This gigantic fen was situated near the Atlantic Ocean, under the shadow of the lofty Mount Atlas.

When Queen Merina ascended the throne, she determined to accomplish mightier deeds than her ancestors. Assembling an army of thirty thousand foot and two thousand horse, dressed in coats of mail made from the skins of large serpents, she passed into Africa, conquered the Atlantides, the Gorgons, and many another nation, and formed an alliance with Orus, King of Egypt, the son of Isis. After making war successfully on the Arabians she conquered Syria and Cilicia, and the tribes around Mount Taurus, who, says Diodorus, "were both men of strong bodies and stout hearts"; marched through Phrygia, and passed along the shores of the Mediterranean, founding several cities, one of which she named after herself, and the others after her principal captains.

Crossing to the Greek Archipelago, where she conquered Lesbos and other isles, Merina founded the
city of Mitylene, and named it after her sister, who
accompanied the expedition.

Shortly after the return of the Amazons to Africa,
Mompsus, a refugee from the court of Lycurgus,
king of Thrace, and Sipylus, a banished Scythian,
invaded the dominions of Merina. The queen was
slain in the first battle, together with many thousand
Amazons; and the rest of her subjects, after bravely
contending in several engagements with the invaders,
retired, it is said, into Lybia.

We also read that Egee, another queen of the African
Amazons, also raised a large army, with which she
invaded Asia. Being opposed by Laomedon, King
of Troy (who was afterwards conquered by Hercules),
she defeated his troops in several actions, and took a
quantity of valuable plunder. While re-passing the
sea a storm arose, and Egee perished with her entire
army.

The nation was finally extirpated by Hercules
when he undertook his journey into Africa, and
erected the famous Pillars.

Herodotus mentions two Libyan tribes, the Mach-
lyes and Auses, dwelling on the shores of Lake
Tritonis, who trained their girls to the use of arms.
Once a year, at the festival of Minerva, their patron-

goddess, the maidens of each tribe formed themselves into two hostile armies, and attacked each
other before the temple with sticks and stones,
contending for the victory with the most desperate
valour. On the conclusion of this *sham* fight, the
most beautiful of the survivors was presented with a
magnificent suit of armour and a sword, and, amidst
the noisiest acclamations from the spectators, escorted
in a chariot triumphantly round the lake.

The Zaveces, another African tribe mentioned
by the same historian, employed their wives and
daughters to drive their war-chariots on the day of
battle, thus placing them in the front of the battle.

From what certain modern travellers have reported,
it would seem that even as lately as the eighteenth
century the legend of the Amazons still held its
ground in various parts of Asia and Africa. Father
Archangel Lamberti, a Neapolitan monk, who
travelled through Mingrelia in the seventeenth
century, was told that a warlike and ruthless nation,
amongst whom were several female warriors, dwelt
somewhere in the neighbourhood of the Caucasus.
They were often at war with the Calmuc Tartars and
the various tribes living near them. Lamberti was
even shown some suits of armour taken from the
corpses of these warlike women, together with their
bows and arrows and brass-spangled buskins.

The Chevalier Chardin (a Huguenot jeweller, knighted by Charles II. of England), in travelling through Persia, between 1663 and 1680, was told that a powerful nation of Amazons dwelt to tho north of the kingdom of Caket. The monarchs of the latter country, which was situated in the neighbourhood of the Caucasus, subjected these Amazons for a time, though they afterwards regained their liberty. The people of the Caucasus, and the Calmucs were always at war with these Amazons, and never sought to make peace or form any treaties, for they knew the warlike women had neither religion, laws, nor honour. Sir John, however, adds that he never met with anybody who had been in their country.

Juan de los Sanctos, an early Portuguese traveller, in speaking of a kingdom named Damut, in Ethiopia, mentions a numerous tribe entirely composed of women, who had adopted (or perhaps retained) the habits of the ancient Amazons. The exercise of arms and the pastime of the chase were their principal occupations in times of peace, but their chief business and pleasure was war. They burnt off the right breast as soon as the girls were old enough to bear it ; and, as a rule, they passed their lives in a state of celibacy, the queen setting a rigid example. Those who married did not rear their male children, but sent them back to the fathers. The neighbouring sovereigns esteemed themselves only too fortunate when they could secure the alliance of this people; and so far from seeking to destroy them, more than once aided them when they were attacked by others. This tribe was finally subjugated, says the Portuguese friar, by the successors of Prester John, the kings of Abyssinia.

## II.

EMIRAMIS is the earliest female warrior of whose existence there is any certainty. But even her history is intermingled with much of fable and idle tradition. The exact period at which she reigned has never been positively determined. The following dates, assigned to her reign by various historians, ancient and modern, as compared by the antiquarian Bryant, show the diversity of opinion amongst chronologists upon the subject.

|  | B.C. |
|---|---|
| According to Syncellus, she lived | 2177 |
| Petavius makes the time | 2060 |
| Helvicus | 2248 |
| Eusebius | 1984 |
| Mr. Jackson | 1964 |
| Archbishop Usher | 1215 |
| Philo Biblius Sanchoniathan (apud Euseb.) | 1200 |
| Herodotus (about) | 713 |

" What credit," indignantly asked the learned Bryant, " can be given to the history of a person, the time of whose life cannot be ascertained within 1535 years ? "

The early life of this famous woman is enveloped in one of those mythological legends in which the ancients loved to shroud the origin of their heroes and heroines. According to tradition she was the natural daughter of Derceto, a Philistine goddess, and while yet a babe, was left to perish by her cruel mother in a wood near Ascalon, in Syria. But, as Romulus and Remus were suckled by a wolf, so doves came and fed the future queen. The birds were observed and followed by the neighbouring peasants; and Simma, or Sisona, chief shepherd of the Assyrian king, having no children of his own, adopted the babe, and gave her the name of

Semiramis, a Syrian word signifying doves, or pigeons.

At the early age of thirteen or fourteen, Semiramis was married to Menon, one the principal officers of the king, who saw her at the hut of Sisona while inspecting the royal flocks. Captivated by her surpassing beauty and charming conversation, Menon induced her to return with him to Nineveh, the capital. For some months she was kept a close prisoner in her husband's palace; but her influence soon ruled paramont, and all restraints were removed. Two or three years passed thus, during which time Semiramis bore her husband two sons, Hypates and Hydaspes.

When Ninus invaded Media, Semiramis, who only waited for some opportunity to distinguish herself, insisted upon accompanying her husband, who, as one of the principal courtiers, held an important command in the invading army. The campaign was at first an uninterrupted series of successes. One city fell after another before the Assyrian hosts. But the army was suddenly checked in its onward career of victory before the impregnable walls of Bactria. The city was defended with such obstinate bravery that Ninus at last resolved to retreat. But Semiramis presented herself before the assembled council of war, proposed an assault on the citadel, and offered to lead, in person, the storming party.

When the decisive moment arrived, Semiramis
proved herself fully equal to the emergency. Amidst
vollies of arrows and showers of stones, before which
the bravest men turned pale, she led the forlorn hope
to the foot of the citadel. Animating all by her
courage, shaming cowards by the thought that a
young and lovely woman was sharing, nay, braving,
the same dangers as themselves, the intrepid heroine
rushed up the scaling ladder, and was the first to
reach the battlements. A struggle ensued, short,
but fierce, and in a few moments the golden standard
of Assyria floated from the walls. The capital of
Media had fallen.

The king, violently smitten with love for the brave
girl, earnestly besought her husband to give her up.
He even offered his own royal sister, Sosana, in exchange. But promises and threats were alike vain;
and Ninus, in a fury, cast Menon into prison. Here,
after being deprived of sight, the wretched husband
terminated his existence with his own hands.

Ninus married the young widow; and after their
return to Nineveh, she bore him a son called Ninyas.

'Tis said Ninus paid very dear for his marriage.
Semiramis, by her profuse liberality, soon attached
the leading courtiers to her interest. She then
solicited the king, with great importunity, to place
the supreme power in her hands for five days. Ninus
at last yielded to her entreaties; and, as his reward,

was cast into prison, and put to death,—either immediately, or after languishing some years.

To cover the meanness of her origin, and to immortalise her name, Semiramis now applied her mind to great enterprises. If she did not, as some suppose, found Babylon the Great, she adorned it with beautiful and imposing edifices, and made it worthy to be called "the Golden City."

Not satisfied with the vast empire left by Ninus, she enlarged it by successive conquests. Great part of Ethiopia succumbed to her power; and during her stay in this country she consulted the Oracle of Jupiter-Ammon as to how long she had to live. The answer was, that she should not die until conspired against by her son; and that, after her death, part of Asia would pay her divine honours.

Her last and most famous expedition was the war with India. For this campaign she raised an army of more than ordinary dimensions. Ctesias puts down the number at three million foot, fifty thousand horse, and war-chariots in proportion; but this is, no doubt, a slight exaggeration. The chief strength of the Indians lay in their countless myriads of elephants. Semiramis, unable to procure these animals in sufficient numbers, caused several thousand camels to be accoutred like elephants.

Shahbrohates, King of India, on receiving intelligence of her hostile approach, sent ambassadors to inquire her motive for invading his dominions. She returned a haughty answer ; and, on reaching the Indus, she erected a bridge of boats and attempted to cross. The passage was disputed, and although the Indians at last retreated, the victory was more disastrous to the Assyrians than many a defeat.

But Semiramis, carried away by the blind infatuation which guided all her movements in this war, marched into the heart of the country. The king, who fled deceitfully to bring about a second engagement further from the river, faced about, and the two armies again closed in deadly combat. The counterfeit elephants could not long sustain the attack of the genuine animals, who, crushing every obstacle under foot, soon scattered the Assyrian army. Semiramis performed prodigies of bravery to rally her broken forces, and fought with as little regard for her own safety as though she had been the meanest soldier in the army. Shahbrohates, perceiving the queen engaged in the thick of the fight, rode forward and twice wounded her. The rout soon became general, and the royal heroine, convinced at last that nothing further could be done, gave the rein to her horse, whose swiftness soon placed her beyond the reach of the enemy.

On reaching the Indus a scene of the most terrible disorder ensued. In the wild terror which possessed the minds of all, officers and soldiers crowded together

on to the bridge, without the slightest regard for rank
or discipline.  Thousands were trampled under foot,
crushed to death, or flung into the river.  When
Semiramis and all who could save themselves had
crossed over, the bridge was destroyed.  The Indian
king, in obedience to an oracle, ordered his troops not
to cross the river in pursuit.

Semiramis was the only sovereign amongst the
ancients, except Alexander the Great, who ever
carried a war beyond the Indus.

Some time after her return to Babylon, the queen
discovered that her son, Ninyas, was conspiring
against her.  Remembering now the oracle of
Jupiter-Ammon, and believing that her last days
were approaching, Semiramis voluntarily abdicated
the throne.  Some chroniclers give a different version
of the story, relating that the queen was slain by
her son, and this latter account, though disbelieved
by most historians, is the popular story.

Semiramis lived sixty-two years, out of which she
reigned forty-two.  It is said the Athenians afterwards worshipped her under the form of a dove.

The early lives of Harpalyce and Atalanta, the first
known female warriors who were natives of Greece,
resemble in some respects that of Semiramis.  It
appears to have been a favourite custom, during the
primitive ages, to have children nursed by birds or

beasts. Harpalyce, daughter of Harpalycus, or Lycurgus, king of the Amymnæans, in Thrace, having lost her mother during infancy, was fed with the milk of cows and horses. Her father trained her in every manly and warlike exercise, riding, racing, hurling the dart, using the bow and arrow. By-and-by she became a mighty huntress; and soon the opportunity came for her to prove herself a brave soldier and a skilful commander. The Getes, or Myrmidones of Thessaly invaded the dominions of King Lycurgus, defeated his best troops and made him prisoner. Directly Harpalyce learned this news she hastily called together an army, placed herself at its head, and falling on the foe, put them to flight and rescued her father.

Lycurgus endeavoured to cure the Thracians of their drunken habits, and caused all the vines in his dominions to be rooted up, whereby he brought about a general insurrection, and was compelled to fly for safety to the isle of Naxos, where he went mad and committed suicide. Harpalyce turned brigand and haunted the forests of Thrace. She was so swift of foot that the fleetest horses could not overtake her once she began running. At last, however, she fell into a snare set by some shepherds, who put the royal bandit to death.

Atalanta, too, was likewise bereft of a mother's care. Her father, Jasus or Jasion, unwilling to rear the

babe, yet not sufficiently inhuman to see her slaughtered before his eyes, left her to her fate on
Mount Parthenius, the highest mountain in Peloponnesus. Close by was the cave of an old she-bear
who had been robbed of her cubs. In place of
devouring the babe, the savage brute adopted it, and
brought up the girl as her own daughter. Orson-
like, the girl learned many of the habits of her
shaggy nurse. But, she also, through constant
exercise, acquired marvellous dexterity in using the
bow and arrow; and with this weapon she once
slew the Centaurs Rhœcus and Hylæus.

Atalanta was one of those brave warriors who
sailed in the Argonautic expedition, B.C. 1263; and
throughout the voyage she earned the praises of her
comrades by her bravery and military skill. After
her return to Greece she assisted in the chase of the
Calydonian boar, a savage brute of monster size
who was ravaging Ætolia. She was the first to
wound this beast; hence Meleager awarded her
the first prize. His uncles, jealous of the honour
thus conferred upon a woman, endeavoured to wrest
the trophies from her, and in the scuffle which ensued,
Meleager unfortunately slew both his uncles.

This heroine must not be confounded with another
Atalanta, daughter of Schœnus, King of Scyrus,
famous for her marvellous skill in running, and for
the stratagem of the three golden apples by which
she was at last defeated.

It would seem that no Grecian or Trojan heroines distinguished themselves during the siege of Troy; though it is not unlikely that many of the Greek soldiers were secretly accompanied by their wives. When Æneas landed in Italy, a few years after the fall of Troy, he found, amongst the sovereigns confederated against him, Camilla, the Amazon queen of the Volscians, renowned for her high courage, her beauty, and her swiftness in running. Virgil says that she outstripped the winds in speed, and could have skimmed over the topmost stalks of standing corn, or along the surface of the ocean, without leaving a trace of her footsteps.

From childhood she was dedicated by her father, King Metabus, to the service of Diana, and trained in martial exercises. She grew so fond of the chase, that even after the death of her father, she preferred leading the semi-barbarous life of a wild huntress to the prospect of domestic happiness as the wife of a Tuscan noble.

She joined Turnus, King of the Rutulians, with a squadron of horse and a body of foot, equipped in bronze armour. Followed by her retinue of warlike maidens, she bore a prominent part in a battle fought near the walls of Latium. But after spreading death and terror on every side, she was herself slain by a Tuscan chief.

Virgil's description of her death is one of the most beautiful passages in the Æneid.

Cyrus, one of the greatest conquerors the world has ever seen, some say met his first and last defeat a the hands of a female general. Many historians describe him as dying peaceably in his bed, sur-rounded by his family; but others relate that, still thirsting for fresh conquests, he cast his eyes, in an unlucky moment, on the land of the Massagetæ, a warlike people governed by Queen Tomyris, a widow, and a woman possessing both courage and energy. Her country extended beyond the broad stream of the Araxes, to the Caucasus. The Massagetæ were a savage, hardy race, resembling the Scythians in their mode of like. Agriculture was neglected, and they subsisted entirely upon their cattle and the fish supplied by the Araxes. Though they had nothing to lose by a change, this nation was devotedly attached to its freedom; suffering death rather than the loss of liberty, and resolutely opposing every invader.

It was against this indomitable race that Cyrus marched, at the head of two hundred thousand men, B.C. 529. By means of a stratagem he was at first successful. Knowing the Massagetæ to be ignorant of Persian delicacies and the flavour of wine, he spread out a banquet, accompanied with flowing goblets of

wine; and, leaving a few hundreds of his worst soldiers
to guard the camp, retired to some distance. When
the Massagetæ, commanded by Spargapises, nephew
of Tomyris, had taken the camp, they feasted and
drank, till, overcome by drunkenness and sleep, they
afforded an easy victory to Cyrus. The greater
number, including Spargapises, were made prisoners,
or slain.

However, so far from despairing, Tomyris collected
the rest of her forces, and having led the Persians
into a narrow pass, attacked them with such fury
that they were all slain, together with the king.
Justin says "there was not one man left to carry
the news home;" but as the news *did* somehow find
its way home, that fact is doubtful.

The body of Cyrus was discovered after considerable search. Tomyris ordered the head to be cut off
and flung into a vessel full of human blood.

"Satisfy thyself now with blood," cried she, ex-
ulting over her dead foe, "which thou didst always
thirst after, yet could never satisfy thy appetite."

A few years prior to the invasion of Greece by
Xerxes, Cleomenes, King of Lacedæmon, who arro-
gated to his state the first rank in Greece, went to
war with the people of Argos. Having learned from
an oracle that he would be victorious, the Spartan
king without loss of time invaded the Argeian

territories, and routed the enemy in a sanguinary battle at Sepeia. Those Argives who escaped death on the battle-field took refuge in a grove sacred to Argus, their hero; where, however, they were surrounded and burnt alive by the enemy. Upwards of six thousand, the flower and strength of Argos, perished that day. Cleomenes marched direct to the city, which, decimated, almost depopulated though it was, made a gallant defence.

There dwelt in the city a beautiful girl named Telesilla, famous throughout the land as a lyric poetess. Inspired by patriotism, she addressed the Argive women and incited them to defend their homes. The call was responded to with enthusiasm. Armed with weapons from the temples, or from private dwellings, the women of Argos, headed by Telesilla, ascended the walls, and compensated by their courage for the dearth of male warriors.

The Spartans were repulsed; and Cleomenes, afraid of being reproached, even if successful, with fighting against helpless women and timid girls, commanded a retreat.

Demeratus, Cleomenes' partner in the throne, is said by some historians to have accompanied this expedition; and they relate that whilst Cleomenes was besieging the walls, Demeratus attacked the Pamphyliacum, or Citadel, whence he was driven with great loss by Telesilla and her companions.

This, however, is acknowledged to be mere tradition, for Herodotus says that the two kings, having quarrelled some years previously, never engaged together in the same war.

Grote, for an even better reason, disbelieves the entire story, which, he says, "is probably a myth, generated by the desire to embody in detail the dictum of the oracle a little before, about 'the female conquering the male.'" Without for a moment denying that the Argeian women could or would have achieved the great deeds ascribed to them, he doubts their having done so, because, says he, the siege never took place at all.

Great honours, so runs the legend, were paid to Telesilla and her brave companions, many of whom fell in the conflict. A statue of the poetess was erected by the grateful citizens and placed in the Temple of Venus.

The terrible danger of the Persian invasion caused all the internal wranglings and disputes of the Greeks to be hushed for a time. In the year B.C. 480, the Great King declared war on the (temporarily) united states of Greece, and sailed thither with a gigantic and overwhelming army and navy. Amongst the tributary sovereigns who followed him in this expedition was Artemisia, Queen of Caria. She was daughter of King Lygdamis, and her hus-

band, the late king, having died while her son was
a minor, Artemisia conducted, *pro. tem.*, the government of Halicarnassus, Cos, Nisiras, and Calydne.
Though she brought only five ships to the Greek
war, they were almost the lightest and best equipped
of any in the fleet.

Herodotus says that amongst all the Persian
commanders, naval or military, there was not one
who gave the king such good advice as this heroine;
but King Xerxes was not at that time wise enough
to profit by her counsels. She was the only one
who had the courage to raise her voice against the
proposed sea-fight at Salamis, which Xerxes was
resolved to risk.

As the Carian queen foretold, the Persians were
defeated. Yet, though she openly disapproved of
the battle, Artemisia behaved most gallantly throughout. The Athenians, indignant that a woman should
dare to appear in arms against them, offered ten
thousand drachmas for her capture, alive or dead.
The way she escaped displayed great presence of
mind, though it also showed how unscrupulous she
was in the choice of stratagems. Closely pursued
by an Athenian ship (commanded by Aminias of
Pallene, the brother of Æschylus), escape seemed
impossible. But with her customary decision of
mind, the queen hung out Grecian colours, and
turned her arms against a Persian vessel. This cost

her no feelings of regret, for on board the ship was Damasithymus, King of Calynda, with whom she had some private quarrel. Her pursuers, seeing her send a Persian ship to the bottom of the sea, concluded that she belonged to their navy, and so gave up the pursuit.

Xerxes, from an elevated post on shore, saw the disgraceful flight of his own navy, together with the bravery of Artemisia. When he could no longer doubt that it was she who performed such gallant deeds, he exclaimed, in astonishment, that the men had behaved like women, while the women had displayed the courage of men.

Like most warlike leaders, Artemisia was not at all scrupulous as to the means employed, provided the end answered her expectations. Wishing to possess herself of Latmus, a small city which lay temptingly near to Halicarnassus, she placed her troops in ambush, and under pretence of celebrating the feast of Cybele in a wood consecrated to that goddess, she repaired thither with a grand procession, accompanied by drums and trumpets. The people of Latmus ran out in crowds to witness the show, while Artemisia's troops took possession of the city.

The ultimate fate of Artemisia proves how true it is that "love rules the court, the camp, the grove." She fell violently in love with a native of Abydos, a young man named Dardanus; but her passion was not reciprocated. To punish his disdain, she first put out his eyes, and then took the noted " Lover's Leap " from the promontory Leucas—now Santa Maura.

Artemisia II., who lived more then one hundred and thirty years after the former heroine, has frequently been confounded with her, as both were queens of Caria. The second of that name was daughter of King Hecatomus, and is principally famous for the honours which she paid to the memory of her husband, Mausolus, to whom she erected a magnificent tomb at Halicarnassus, which monument was afterwards reckoned as one of the Seven Wonders of the World.

Most writers represent Artemisia as plunged in tears during her widowhood; but there are some who, on the contrary, declare that she made some important conquests at that time. Vitruvius relates that the Rhodians, indignant that a woman should reign over Caria, despatched a fleet to Halicarnassus to dethrone Artemisia. The queen commanded the citizens to appear on the walls directly the Rhodians came in sight, and to express, by shouts and clapping of hands, their readiness to surrender. The enemy, falling into the trap, disembarked, and went with all haste to the city, leaving their ships without even one man to guard them

Artemisia came out with her squadron from the little port, entered the great harbour, and seized the Rhodian vessels. Putting her own men on board she sailed to Rhodes, where the people, seeing their own ships return adorned with laurel-wreaths, received them with every demonstration of joy. No resistance was offered to the landing; and Artemisia seized the city, putting to death the leaders of the people.

She caused a trophy to be erected, and set up two statues—one representing the city of Rhodes, and the other an image of herself, branding the former figure with a red-hot iron. Vitruvius says the Rhodians were forbidden by their religion to destroy this memorial; so they surrounded it by a lofty building which concealed it from view.

Her death, which took place the same year (B.C. 351) probably reinstated the Rhodians in their liberty.

During the reign of Artaxerxes Nmenon, King of Persia, and brother of Cyrus the younger, the province of Æolia was governed—under the authority of Pharnabasus, satrap of Asia Minor—by Zenis the Dardanian. When the latter died, Mania, his widow, went to Pharnabasus with magnificent presents, leading a body of troops, and begged of him not to deprive her of the government. Pharnabasus allowed her to retain the province, and he had no reason to regret it. Mania acquitted herself with all the prudence and energy which could have been expected from the most experienced ruler. In addition to the customary tributes, she added magnificent presents; and when Pharnabasus visited her province, she entertained him with greater splendour than any of the other governors throughout Asia Minor. She followed him in all his military campaigns, and was of great assistance not only with her troops, but by her advice. She was a regular attendant at all his councils, and her suggestions contributed to the success of more than one enterprise. The satrap knew how to estimate her merit; and the Governess of Æolia was treated with greater distinction than any of her fellow-governors.

Her army was in better condition than that of any neighbouring province; she even maintained a body of Greek soldiers in her pay. Not content with the cities committed to her care, she made new conquests; amongst others, Larissa, Amaxita, and Colona, which belonged to the Mysians and Pisidians. In every war she took the command in person, and from her war-chariot decreed rewards and punishments.

The only enemies she possessed were in her own family circle. Midias, her son-in-law, thinking it a reproach on him that a woman should command where he was subordinate, strangled her and her son, B.C. 399, and seized two fortresses in which she had secured her treasures. The other cities of Æolia at once declared against him; and he did not very long enjoy the fruits of his crime. Dercyllidas, commander of the Greek forces in Asia, arrived at this juncture. All the fortresses in the province surrendered, either voluntarily or by compulsion; and Midias was deprived of the possessions for which he had stained his hands in the blood of his relatives.

Cratesipolis was the wife of Alexander, the son of one of Alexander the Great's captains.

On the sudden death of Alexander the Great, his posthumous son and his half-brother were placed on the throne, under the regency of Perdiccas, the most talented of Alexander's captains. However, the generals soon began to quarrel among themselves; two years later, Perdiccas was assassinated, and the regency conferred on Antipater, governor of Macedonia and Greece. The latter, on his death-bed, bestowed the office of regent and the government of the provinces on Polysperchon, the eldest survivor of all the captains who had followed Alexander to India. Cassander, the son of Antipater, indignant at being set aside, went to war with the new regent.

Alexander, the son of Polysperchon, was possessed of great military talent, and his father confided to him the defence of Peloponnesus. Cassander, knowing the abilities of Alexander, offered him the government of Peloponnesus, and the command of the troops stationed there if he would join the faction of the malcontents. The offer was accepted ; Alexander established his head quarters at Sicyon. At the head of his troops he gained several victories. Cratesipolis, his wife, was the idol of the soldiers. They regarded her, and justly, as a woman who possessed the spirit of a hero and the talents of a great general. She interested herself in all their affairs —appeased all their differences, and did not disdain to think of their wants and their pleasures. She consoled those who were sad, relieved those who were in want, and strove to make all happy. Frequently she accompanied Alexander in his expeditions, and was as much respected by the officers as beloved by the privates.

Alexander held his governorship for only a few months. The citizens of Sicyon, furious, and groaning under the yoke imposed upon them, conspired against their rulers. The governor was slain by Alexion and some companions who pretended to be Alexander's friends. The soldiers, who were setting out on an expedition, seized with terror when they saw their leader fall, fled in all directions.

Cratesipolis gave way neither to grief nor despair. Rallying the broken forces, she assumed the command, and soon restored order and discipline. The Sicyonians, who never suspected that a woman could take the command of the army, rose in rebellion, and barred the city gates. Cratesipolis, enraged as much at the insult as at the treachery with which they had slain her husband, laid siege to Sicyon, routed the insurgents in a hotly-contested battle, and took the city by storm (B.C. 317), when, by her command, thirty of the ringleaders were crucified.

Having assuaged her thirst for revenge, Cratesipolis entered Sicyon in triumph, and assumed the government. Appeasing all the troubles caused by the rebellion, she ruled with such wisdom and prudence as to excite the admiration of all. To the last she kept up a large and well-disciplined army, always ready at a moment's notice to set forth on an expedition. The soldiers, whose love and reverence had been increased by the courage with which she had acted during the insurrection, would, any of them, have gladly sacrificed his own life to save hers.

Arsinoe, Queen of Egypt, was the wife of Ptolemy Philopater. She was a brave as well as prudent woman, and accompanied her husband when he invaded Syria, B.C. 217. In the battle of Raphia she rode up and down through the ranks, exhorting the soldiers to behave manfully during the fight. She remained beside her husband during the heat of the action; and by her presence she greatly contributed to the victory gained by the Egyptians.

## III.

PONTUS, in Cappadocia, the *ci-devant* home
of the Amazons, passed through many
changes and vicissitudes as time rolled
on. Under Cyrus and his successors,
Cappadocia was divided into two distinct provinces,
whose governors made themselves finally independent
of Persia, and ruled as kings till the days of Alexander. After the death of the great Macedonian,
Pontus was not long regaining its independence:

increasing rapidly in power and extent till the days
of Mithridates the Great, who made it one of the chief
empires of the East.

This ambitious monarch, believing himself a second
Alexander, cared for nothing but war; and through
his bravery and his obstinacy, he contrived to make
himself one of the most formidable rivals Rome ever
had to cope with. Hypsicrates was his favourite
wife—like most Oriental monarchs, he had more
than one; and in respect of personal courage, she
was worthy to be the companion of the royal tiger.
They were romantically attached to one another;
Mithridates, ruthless towards others, was loving and
tender to his favourite sultana. She accompanied
him in many of his perilous expeditions, and fought
by his side in more than one battle. For this reason,
her name, properly Hypsicratia, was changed to
Hypsicrates; thus altering it from feminine to masculine, on account of her manly courage. Besides
being valiant, she was exceedingly beautiful and
highly accomplished, as a queen should be.

After the defeat of Mithridates by Lucullus, the
gourmand, on the plains of Cabiræ, B.C. 71, the unfortunate monarch sent a messenger to the ladies of his
court, enjoining them to die by their own hands rather
than fall alive into those of the Romans. All obeyed
save Hypsicrates. Though she feared death as
little as any among them, yet could she not bear

even this temporary separation from her lord. Mounting a swift steed, she overtook the king, after encountering and surmounting innumerable difficulties; and by her presence and counsel she restored to him his former energy and strength of mind.

Five years later (B.C. 66), Mithridates fought a battle with Pompey the Great on the banks of the Euphrates. Hypsicrates appeared in the dress of a Persian soldier, and, mounted on a charger, fought beside the king so long as the action lasted. However, the battle was not of long duration. The barbarians were afraid to await the shock of the iron legions, and fled in wild terror. The Romans ruthlessly slaughtered the fugitives; ten thousand were slain on the field, and the camp fell into the hands of the victors.

Mithridates and his brave queen, placing themselves at the head of eight hundred chosen horsemen, cut their way, sword in hand, through the ranks of the foe. But the eight hundred quickly dispersed, and left the king with only three followers, one of whom was Hypsicrates. She attended him during his flight, grooming his horse, and enduring great hardships through fatigue and want of food. At last they reached a fortress, where lay the royal treasures. Here Mithridates gave to each a dose of strong poison to be taken in case of dire necessity. But whether Hypsicrates finally swallowed the fatal potion, or by what death she passed from the world, historians have not told us.

Cleopatra, the beautiful and ambitious queen of Egypt, was at all times desirous to acquire renown as a great warrior. But she possessed neither the courage nor the prudence necessary for those who seek the laurel-wreath. She was too fond of her ease to take the command of an expedition, unless the occasion was one which rendered her presence absolutely necessary.

She first appeared as a warrior in the year B.C. 48, when her brother Ptolemy deprived her of her share in the throne. She withdrew to Syria, raised troops there, and re-entered Egypt at the head of her forces shortly after the battle of Pharsalia. Pompey, routed by Cæsar, fled to Egypt, where he was assassinated by order of the king. Scarcely had he breathed his last, when Cæsar landed. He assumed the right to arbitrate between Ptolemy and Cleopatra. The former refused to accept him as referee, and for several weeks the great Cæsar had to contend with the soldiers of the king as well as with the infuriated citizens of Alexandria. However, the war was soon terminated by the defeat and death of Ptolemy; and the crown was bestowed upon Cleopatra.

After the assassination of Julius Cæsar, Cleopatra

declared for the Triumvirs, Antony, Octavius, and
Lepidus. She prepared a powerful fleet, designing to
take the command, and sail to the assistance of
Cæsar's avengers. Violent storms prevented the
squadron from setting out; but some time subse-
quently the queen sailed with a well-equipped fleet
to join the Triumvirs. Again she was frustrated by
the elements. A terrible storm arose, wrecked many
vessels, threw the queen on a bed of sickness, and
compelled the fleet to put back to Alexandria.

This love of warlike display finally caused her
ruin and that of Antony. Against the advice of the
most practised Roman officers, she insisted upon
taking an active part in the war against Octavius.
Before the decisive battle of Actium, Antony was
counselled not to hazard a sea-fight; but the haughty
Egyptian queen, like Xerxes of old, insisted upon it.
So her advice was followed in preference to that of
old and experienced generals.

The battle was fought on the 2nd September,
B.C. 31, at the mouth of the Ambracian Gulf, within
sight of the opposing land armies who were encamped
on each shore anxiously watching the struggle. A
more magnificent sight could not have been seen
than the fleet of Antony; and the most splendid
object in it was the galley of Cleopatra, blazing with
gilding and bright colours, its sails of purple, flags
and streamers floating in the wind. Victory inclined

to neither side till the flight of the Egyptian queen.
Terrified by the horrid din of the fight, though in no
personal danger, she fled from the scene of action,
her example being followed by nearly all the Egyptian
fleet, which numbered sixty ships.  Antony, when he
saw the queen's galley take to flight, forgot everything but her, and precipitately followed.  And thus
he yielded to Cæsar not merely the victory, but the
Sovereignty of the World.

About the time that Cleopatra sat on the throne
of Egypt, the neighbouring kingdom of Ethiopia was
ruled over by another warlike queen, Candace, whose
kingdom comprised that part of the Nile valley,
which, under the name of Meröe, contained numberless towns and cities in a high state of civilization.
Very little is known concerning this queen, save
what we glean from Strabo.  The year before the
battle of Actium, Candace invaded Egypt, and compelled the Roman garrisons of Syene, Elephantine,
and Philæ to surrender.  Caius Petronius, Roman
prefect of Egypt, marched against the Ethiopians,
and routed Candace near Pselcha, after which the victor ravaged great part of Ethiopia.
When Petronius left the country, Candace attacked
the garrison he had left in Premnis.  But directly
the prefect heard of this he returned hastily to
Meröe, again defeated the Ethiopians, and imposed

a heavy tribute on the kingdom. Candace sent an embassy to Octavius, who was then at Samos, suing for peace. The dictator not only granted her prayer, but remitted the tribute levied by Petronius.

The next female sovereign who defied Rome on the battle-field was of a very different stamp from Cleopatra, or even Candace. This was Boadicea, the "British Warrior Queen," the story of whose wrongs and bravery was for centuries a favourite subject with poets. Her name, which has been variously written Boadicea, Boudicea, Bonduca, Vonduca, Voadicea, or Woda, signified " the Woman of the Sword," and in the ancient British or Welsh language is equivalent to Victoria. She was the daughter of Cadalla, King of the Brigantes; and, through her mother, Europeia, daughter of Evanus, King of Scotland, she claimed descent from the kings of Troy and the Ptolemies of Egypt.

Boadicea's career was a sad and a stormy one from first to last. At an early age she was compelled by her step-mother, the wicked, ambitious, Cartismandua, to marry Arviragus, son of that queen by her first husband, King Cymbeline. Arviragus was King of the Iceni, who possessed a great part of Essex, Norfolk, and Cambridgeshire. They are said by Tacitus to have been a rich and powerful nation.

After the queen had presented her lord with a son and two daughters, the Emperor Claudius came to Britain. Arviragus, having suffered several defeats, was compelled to divorce Boadicea, and marry Gwenissa, the emperor's daughter. A general insurrection of the Britons was the result; and the natives, led at first by the famous Caractacus, brother of Boadicea, and ultimately joined by Arviragus himself, were defeated again and again by the Romans. Weary at last of the never-ending struggle, Arviragus and Boadicea accepted very humiliating terms from Vespasian, and were permitted to retain their dominions.

Towards the close of his life Arviragus appears, for some unexplained reason, to have changed his name to Prasutagus. Dreading the rapacity of the Romans, he thought to secure their protection for Boadicea and her two daughters (her son died long before), by making the emperor Nero joint-heir to his dominions. He died A.D. 61. Scarcely had he ceased to breathe, when Catus, the Roman procurator, who commanded in the absence of Suetonius Paulinus, Governor of Britain, annexed the country of the Iceni, siezed the personal effects of the deceased monarch, treated all his relations as prisoners of war, despoiled the wealthier Iceni, imposed heavy taxes upon the poor, and demanded from Boadicea the payment of large sums which her father, Cadalla, had bestowed upon the Romans. Unable to pay, the queen was publicly whipped, and her daughters were treated even more shamefully.

Burning for revenge, Boadicea raised the standard of revolt. She was soon joined by patriots from all parts of Britain. Eighty thousand men, headed by the queen, rushed down like wild beasts on the colonies of Camulodunum (Malden), Colchester, and Verulam (St. Alban's), putting to death, in the first-named city, with every torture they could devise, more than seventy thousand persons of every age. and sex.

Shortly after the destruction of Camulodunum, Boadicea was joined by her brother Corbred, king of Scots. Together they marched to the attack on Colchester. Petilius Cerialis, the conqueror of Batavia, marched out from Verulam at the head of the ninth legion to oppose the victorious Britons. He had lately received from Germany reinforcements, amounting to eight auxiliary cohorts of one thousand horse. A furious battle ensued, resulting in the total defeat of the Romans. Upwards of six thousand Romans and three thousand confederate Britons (their allies) were slain.

Petilius fled with his broken cohorts—for, it is said, not even one foot-soldier escaped the carnage—to his entrenched camp. Catus Decianus, the procurator, was severely wounded in the engage-

ment, and, struck with terror, he continued his pre-
cipitate flight over sea into Gaul.

Suetonius Paulinus, absent at the time on that
expedition which concluded with the massacre of
the Druids in Mona (the Isle of Anglesea), hastened
back to South Britain. With ten thousand men, he
entered London ; but, despite the prayers of the
people, he deserted it at once, and encamped at a
short distance north of the city. Scarcely had he
departed, when Boadicea marched directly on
London, captured it after a slight resistance, and
put the inhabitants to the sword.

For some time Suetonius was afraid to venture on
a battle against a victorious queen commanding a
force so immeasurably superior to his own, amounting, according to Tacitus, to one hundred thousand,
while Dio Cassius raises the number as high as
two hundred and thirty thousand ; while the Romans
could muster scarcely ten thousand. At last an
engagement took place on a wild spot, guarded in
the rear by a dense forest.

Before the battle, Boadicea passed up and
down in her chariot, exhorting the warriors to
avenge her wrongs and those of her daughters.
Dio Cassius has described the British Queen,
as she appeared on that memorable day. She was
a woman of lofty stature, with a noble, severe
expression, and a dazzlingly fair complexion, re-

markable even amongst the British women, who were famous for the whiteness of their skin. Her long yellow hair, floating in the wind, reached almost to the ground. She wore a tunic of various colours, hanging in folds, and over this was a shorter one, confined at the waist by a chain of gold. Round her alabaster neck was a magnificent "torques," or collar of twisted gold-wire. Her hands and arms were uncovered, save for the rings and bracelets which adorned them. A large British mantle surmounted, but did not conceal the rest of her attire.

Suetonius on his side used all his powers of oratory to excite the Romans to do their best, telling them to "despise the savage uproar, the shouts and yells of undisciplined barbarians," amongst whom, he said, "the women out-numbered the men."

The battle was long and obstinately contested; but the steady order of the iron legions triumphed over the savage onslaught of the Britons. The latter were routed with terrible slaughter, leaving, Tacitus says, upwards of eighty thousand dead on the field. The Romans lost only five hundred. "The glory won on this day," adds Tacitus, "was equal to that of the most renowned victories of the ancient Romans."

The exact scene of this engagement has been

variously placed by different writers. Some decide
that Battle-Bridge, King's Cross, marks the spot;
while by others it has been settled as identical with
the ancient camp called Ambresbury Banks, near
Epping. Some even place it at Winchester.

Boadicea, rather than let herself be taken alive,
put an end to her own existence by poison. She
was afterwards interred with due honours by her
faithful adherents.

The two daughters of Boadicea, completely
armed, fought most valiantly in the battle; and
even during the rout of their countrymen they
strove wildly for victory. At last they were made
prisoners, and brought into the presence of Suetonius, who expressed deep sympathy for them, and
spoke with indignation of their oppressors.

The elder princess, by the intervention of Suetonius, was married, some months later, to Marius,
also styled Westmer, son of Arviragus and Gwenissa.
This prince was acknowledged by the Romans as
King of the Iceni, over whom he ruled for many
years. His son Coel was the father of Lucius, the
first Christian king of Britain. Boadicea, the
younger daughter, inherited not only her mother's
name, but her bold, dauntless spirit, and her relent-
less hatred of the Romans. Marius, fearing her
influence over the Iceni, banished her from his
court. She raised a formidable army of Brigantes

and Picts, and sailed to Galloway, which was
occupied by the Romans. Marching in the dead of
the night, she fell on the encampment of the foe
and slew several hundred men. The entire Roman
army would probably have been put to the sword
had not Petilius, the general, ordered his men to
light torches. The Britons were driven off, and
next morning Boadicea was attacked and defeated
in her own camp.

Next day Boadicea marched to Epiake, the
Roman head-quarters in that district, and setting it
on fire, destroyed the garrison. Shortly after this
she was captured in an ambuscade. It is said by
some that the young princess, expecting a horrible
death, followed the example of her mother, and took
poison. Others, however, declare that she was
brought alive into the presence of the Roman commander, who interrogated her respecting the object
of her invasion, when Boadicea, making a spirited
answer, was slain by his guards.

The bravery of Boadicea and her daughters was
not so strange in those days as it might now be.
The British and Caledonian women were, as a rule,
brave and warlike, and invariably followed their
husbands to battle. More than five thousand women
enlisted under the banners of Boadicea, and fought,
many of them, as bravely as the men. Women,
even far advanced in years, marched with their

male relations to the defence of king or country;
and those who did not fight hand to hand with the
foe, peppered him well from a distance with volleys
of stones. To render themselves competent to
share the perils and dangers of the battle-field, the
women, in times of peace, practised the use of arms,
and inured themselves to fatigue and hardship; as
Holinshed says, "never refusing to undergo any
labour or fatigue assigned them by their leader."

The women of Caledonia were equally warlike.
In a curious old book of engravings published in
London during the last century, entitled a "Collection of Dresses of Different Nations, Ancient and
Modern," there are three plates, one of which represents a Caledonian woman, after De Brii, dressed
in a short garment, and armed with masculine
weapons; the other two represent the wife and
daughter of a Pict. The woman Pict is entirely
naked, and is tattooed and painted with stars, rays,
and various similar devices. In one hand she grasps
a lance and in the other two darts. The girl differs
from the mother only in being painted with divers
floral ornaments in lieu of the astronomical adorn-
ments.

The Gallic and German women also, joined frequently in the battles between rival tribes. Philo-
stratus, probably for this reason, speaks of Amazons
living on the shores of the Danube; and in Lucius

Flaccus we also read of German Amazons. The Allemanni, the Marcomanni, the Quadi, and the other warlike tribes who dwelt beyond the Rhine were always accompanied by their wives and daughters whenever they set out on an expedition. During the battle, such of the women as took no share in the action, stood on the outskirts, cheering and encouraging the warriors. More than once a beaten army of Germans was stopped in its flight by the women, and obliged, through very shame, to turn again and confront the enemy. If their side was defeated the German women almost invariably committed suicide on the corpses of their friends. During the wars of Marcus Aurelius with the Marcomanni and Quadi, several women were found amongst the slain, many clad in armour.

Under the patronage of the emperors the combats of Roman matrons in the amphitheatre afforded intense gratification to a pleasure-seeking public. Juvenal, the satirist, regards these female duels from a ludicrous point of view. "What a fine business it would be," he says, " for a man to cry out at an auction of his wife's equipment, ' Who bids up for my wife's boots ? Who'll give most for her corslet, helmet, and gauntlet ? ' "

The Romans, however, often tried to raise amateur corps of female warriors, in imitation of the ancient Amazons, whose warlike deeds were much admired in the imperial city. Suetonius tells us that Nero, when he learned the news of Galba's revolt, dressed up the women of his seraglio as Amazons, arming them with battle-axes and small bucklers, and intending to march at their head against the rebels.

In the third century the Roman empire was in a state of dire confusion. So many governors of provinces and commanders of legions had assumed the purple, with more or less success, in various parts of the world, that at last the Emperor, who was recognised by the senate at Rome, though nominally sovereign of the universe, was, in fact, very little more than ruler of Italy. One of the first to dispute the imperial dignity in Europe was Posthumus, commander of the legions in Gaul. He so far acquired the affections of his soldiers that they proclaimed him Emperor of the West, A.D., 257. His dominion, the capital of which was Cologne, extended over Gaul, Spain, and Britain.

There dwelt in Cologne a noble Roman lady named Victoria. Some say she was the sister of Posthumus. Be that as it may, she persuaded the emperor to raise her son, Victorinus, to the throne, as his colleague ; and when Posthumus was murdered by the soldiers, three years later, Victorinus remained sole emperor of the West. He was a brave soldier and an able general, and reigned over Gaul for about a year longer, when he was slain by the troops, A.D. 269. His eldest son, named after himself, was now proclaimed emperor; but in a few days he, too, fell a victim to the fury of the legions.

An ordinary mind would have sunk beneath this double misfortune; but the " Heroine of the West " was cast in a very different mould from most women. Exceedingly ambitious, she possessed both the courage and the ability to carry out her schemes. Even when her son was living, she held the reins of government. So great was her influence over the legions, they obeyed her behests in everything without a murmur. She passed much of her time amongst them, and received thence the title of Mater Castrorum,—" Mother of the Camp." When her son became emperor, she, as his mother, received the title of Augusta.

Victoria bestowed the vacant throne first on Marius, a distinguished general, who was slain in a few days, and next on Tetricus, the chief noble in Aquitaine, a distant relative of her own. During his absence in Spain she continued to govern the Gallic provinces. Placing herself at the head of the troops, she maintained the authority she had seized against all the armies sent from Rome. Even during the early days of Aurelian's reign, she opposed the imperial forces with the same bold and undaunted spirit, and with equal success.

Very soon Tetricus grew weary of being subordinate to Victoria. The empress, stung by his ingratitude, would have hurled him from the throne to which
she had raised him; but Tetricus took care to
prevent this by causing Victoria to be poisoned,
A.D. 269, a few months after his own accession.

Since the days of Semiramis no female ruler in
ancient times attained so high a pinnacle of great-
ness throughout the East as Zenobia. For more
than five years, unaided, she set the Roman emperors
at defiance, defeated their armies, and laughed equally
at their threats and their underhand machinations.

Septimia Zenobia was an Arab princess, and while
some writers assert that she was a Jewess, the
heroine herself claimed descent, through her father
Amru, from the Ptolemies of Egypt. Truly she was
as beautiful as any Egyptian queen—even the handsome Cleopatra. By some writers she has been
cited as the loveliest woman of her age. An olive
complexion, pearly teeth, large, brilliant, black eyes,
which sparkled alternately with the fire of the heroine
and the sweetness of the loving wife—such were the
charms of her face. Her voice was rich and musical.
She was conversant with Greek, Latin, Syriac, and
Egyptian; and compiled for her own reading an
epitome of Homer. Her tutor in philosophy was the
famous Greek, Cassius Longinus.

Zenobia was a widow, and the mother of a son, Vhaballathus, when she wedded Odenathus, Prince of Palmyra. The latter, however, was a widower, and also the father of a son—Ouarodes, or Herod, a weak and effeminate youth.

Septimius Odenathus, who raised himself by his own genius and the fortune of war, to the sovereignty of the East, was, like his wife, an Arab. He was chief prince of the wild Saracen tribes who dwelt in the Syrian deserts, on the shores of the Euphrates. Odenathus early learned the rudiments of war in the exciting chase of wild beasts—a pastime which, to the last, he never wearied of, and in which he was joined with equal ardour by Zenobia. Together the royal pair, during the intervals of peace, hunted lions, panthers, or bears, through the woods and deserts of Syria.

When the emperor Valerian was captured and flayed alive by Sapor, King of Persia, A.D. 260, Odenathus marched, at the head of an Arab host, against the Persians, defeated them near Antioch, compelled them to retreat, beat them again on the banks of the Euphrates, and finally drove them across the river; capturing, in the first battle, the greater part of the wives and treasures of Sapor.

Zenobia accompanied her husband in this, as in all his subsequent expeditions, and bravely seconded his efforts. She proved herself as good a soldier as

any, and endured, with the utmost fortitude, the
same hardships as the meanest there.  Disdaining
the use of a covered carriage, she frequently marched
several miles at the head of the troops.

Pursued closely by Odenathus and Zenobia, Sapor
fled through Mesopotamia, suffering many defeats,
losing towns and cities, and at last took refuge in
Ctesiphon, his capital, where the victors besieged
him for some months.

The Roman senate recognised the deeds of Odenathus by granting him the title of Augustus, A.D. 263.
In the following year the royal pair undertook a
second expedition against Sapor.  New triumphs
were added to the glories of the last campaign.  The
Persian king was once more forced to take refuge in
Ctesiphon, which would no doubt have fallen had
not the incursion of a horde of Scythian Goths into
Syria compelled Odenathus to raise the siege.

Surrounding nations soon learned to respect the
brave prince of Palmyra and his no less warlike
consort.  Even Sapor, humiliated though he had
been, was glad, not merely to make peace, but to
join in close alliance with his conquerors, who were
threatened by the underhand machinations of the
contemptible emperor Gallienus.  But the brilliant
career of Odenathus was unexpectedly brought to a
close by the hand of his nephew, who, believing himself insulted by the monarch, assassinated him,

together with his son Herod, at a banquet in the city of Emesa, A.D. 267.

The murderer gained nothing but the empty pleasure of revenge. Scarcely had he assumed the title of Augustus ere he was sacrificed by the royal widow to the memory of her husband, though some historians have accused her of being an accomplice in the double murder. Zenobia was proclaimed queen; and, passing over Timolaus and Herennius, her sons by Odenathus, she arrayed Vhaballathus in the purple, and showed him to the troops as their emperor.

With the death of Odenathus ceased that authority granted him as a personal favour by the emperor and senate of Rome; and Gallienus despatched an army to dethrone Zenobia. But the queen soon compelled the Roman general to retreat into Europe with the loss of both army and reputation. Zenobia governed the East for more than five years; and by successive conquests she extended her dominions from the Euphrates to the Mediterranean and the borders of Bithynia; and added, besides, the land of the Ptolemies. Her power became so great that the warlike Claudius II., who succeeded Gallienus, was satisfied that while he was occupied in the defence of Italy from the Goths and Germans, Zenobia should assert the dignity of the Roman power in the East.

Palmyra, the capital of the warrior queen, almost
rivalled the Eternal City in the magnificence of its
temples, its mansions, its public monuments, and
the luxury of its citizens. It became the great centre
of commerce between Europe and India, and its
merchants grew wealthy through the trade of East
and West. Arcades of lofty palms shadowed its
streets of marble palaces; purling fountains, fed by
icy springs, rendered it a perfect Elysium in the
midst of burning arid sands. Schools, museums,
libraries, fostered by the care of Zenobia, encouraged
and aided the arts and literature.

At last the stern, the inflexible Aurelian ascended
the throne of the Cæsars. Firmly resolved to rid the
empire of every usurper, great or small, he began by
re-conquering Gaul and making prisoner the Western
ursurper, Tetricus. He then passed into Asia, A.D.
272, when his presence alone was sufficient to bring
back Bithynia to its allegiance. Of course Zenobia
did not indolently permit an invader to approach
within a hundred miles of her capital without taking
measures to arrest his progress. She marched with
all her forces to oppose him ; but was signally defeated
in two battles, the first near Antioch, the second near
Emesa. In both engagements the queen animated
the soldiers by her presence, though the actual command devolved on Zabdas, the conqueror of Egypt.
The latter, Zenobia's principal general, has been by

many supposed to have been Zabba, the queen's sister; this, however, is mere surmise.

After the second defeat, Zenobia was unable to raise a third army. She retired within the walls of her capital, prepared to make a gallant defence, and boldly declared that her reign and her life should end together.

Aurelian arrived before Palmyra, after a toilsome march over the sandy desert which separated the city from Antioch. His proposals being rejected with scorn, he was obliged to begin the siege; and, while superintending the operations, he was wounded by a dart.

" The Roman people," he wrote in a letter, " speak with contempt of the war which I am waging against a woman. They are ignorant both of the character and of the power of Zenobia. It is impossible to enumerate her warlike preparations of stones, of arrows, and of every species of missile weapons. Every part of the walls is provided with two or three balistæ, and artificial fires are thrown from her military engines. The fear of punishment has armed her with a desperate courage."

Zenobia was at first supported in her determined resistance by the hope that the Roman army, having no means of getting provisions, would soon be compelled to retreat, and also by the expectation that Persia would come to her aid. Disappointed in both calculations, she mounted her swiftest dromedary and fled towards the Euphrates. But the Roman light cavalry pursued, and soon overtook the queen, who was brought back prisoner. Palmyra surrendered almost immediately after, and was treated with un-expected clemency by the victor.

The courage of Zenobia entirely deserted her when she heard the angry cries of the soldiers, who clamoured for her immediate execution. She threw the entire guilt of her obstinate resistance upon her friends and counsellors, and the celebrated Longinus, amongst others, fell a victim to the emperor's rage.

Vhaballathus, the only surviving son of Zenobia, withdrew into Armenia, where he ruled over a small principality granted him by Aurelian.

When the emperor returned to Rome, in the following year (A.D. 274), he celebrated, after the manner of Roman conquerors, a magnificent triumph in honour of his many victories over the Goths, the Alemanni, Tetricus, and Zenobia. Elephants, royal tigers, panthers, bears, armed gladiators, military standards, and war-chariots passed in succession. But the great object of attention was the Eastern queen, who, completely laden with golden fetters, a gold chain, supported by a slave, round her neck, her limbs bending beneath the weight of the jewels with which she was decked, was compelled to precede, on foot, the triumphal car in which, not many months previously, she had hoped to enter the gates of Rome as a conqueror.

After the conclusion of his triumph, Aurelian presented Zenobia with an elegant villa at Tibur (or Tivoli), about twenty miles from the capital; and here she passed the rest of her days as a Roman matron. She died about the year 300. Her daughters married into wealthy and noble families; some say, indeed, that Aurelian espoused one of them; and the family was not extinct even in the fifth century. Baronius supposes Zenobius, Bishop of Florence, in the days of Saint Ambrose, to have been one of the great queen's descendants.

Amongst the numberless captives—Sarmatians, Alemanni, Goths, Vandals, Gauls, Franks, Dacians, Syrians, Arabs, Egyptians—who unwillingly graced the triumph of Aurelian, were ten Gothic women, captured in a battle between the Goths and Romans when the emperor was driving the barbarians out of Italy. Each party was distinguished in the procession by its own, or by some fancy name; these Gothic females were designated "Amazons." Besides these prisoners, many Gothic women and girls, in male attire, had been found dead on the field of battle.

Hunila, or Hunilda, one of these Gothic women, was afterwards married to Bonosus, a wealthy and influential Roman general, Governor of Rhætia.

She was admired and distinguished amongst her
new friends for her beauty, wit, and virtue. But the
*ci-devant* Amazon kept up communications with her
own countrymen ; and Bonosus, promised assistance
by his wife's relations, assumed the purple. For a
few months his authority extended over Gaul, Spain
and Britain ; but at last he was conquered by the
Emperor Probus. To avoid falling into the hands
of the victor, he put an end to his own life by hanging ; whereupon some wit, alluding to his favourite
vice (for Bonosus, they say, could drink as much as
ten strong men) remarked that "there hung a bottle,
not a man."

Probus spared the life of Hunila, and granted her
an annual pension for the rest of her days ; he permitted her sons to enjoy their paternal estate.

Mavia, Queen of Pharan, another of those troublesome women who defied the Roman emperors, was
by birth a Roman, and by education a Christian.
When very young she was carried away by a troop
of Arabs, who brought her to their prince, Obedien,
King of Pharan. The latter, who was himself a
Christian, charmed by the beauty of his captive,
made her his wife. At his death Mavia became sole
ruler of Pharan. Placing herself at the head of a
numerous army, A.D. 373, she invaded Palestine, and
advancing as far as Phœnicia, defeated the forces of

the emperors Valentinian, Valens, and Gratian in a series of battles extending over some months. The Roman governor of Phœnicia, unable to make head against the invader, was compelled to seek assistance of the general commanding the Eastern emperor's forces. The latter came speedily to his aid, and after bragging much and loudly of what he would do, engaged in battle with Mavia. He was signally beaten, his army cut to pieces, and he had to fly ignominiously.

After this victory the Queen of Pharan gained many another battle, and she proved herself so dangerous an opponent that the Romans were compelled to sue for peace. Peace was at last concluded, on the condition (dictated by Mavia) that the anchorite Moses should be sent as bishop to Pharan. Having thus destroyed idolatry in Pharan, the queen remained for the rest of her days in friendly relationship with the Romans, to one of whom, Count Victor, she gave her daughter in marriage.

Towards the close of the fourth century, one of the Sapors, King of Persia, invaded Armenia, which for many years previously had maintained its independence. He was resolutely opposed by King Tiranus and his wife Pharandsem, or Olympias ; but after valiantly defending his throne for nearly four years, Tiranus was deserted by his nobles and compelled to surrender.

Armenia was once more reduced into a Persian province, and divided between two of Sapor's favourites. The city of Artogerassa was the only stronghold which still dared to resist the Persians. It was defended by Pharandsem. The Persians were surprised and routed under the walls by a bold and concerted sortie of the besieged; but the former were constantly reinforced, while the latter steadily diminished in numbers, through famine and disease, rather than by the weapons of the foe. After a siege of fourteen months the city was compelled to surrender. Pharandsem, with her own hand, flung open the gates, when she was seized by the victors, and, by order of Sapor, impaled.

## IV.

THE ARABS—Henda, Wife of Abu Sofian, an Arab Chief
—Forka, an Arabian Lady—Women of Yemaumah—Arab and
Greek heroines at the Siege of Damascus—Khaullah—Prefect
of Tripoli's Daughter—Ayesha, Widow of the Prophet—Cahina
the Sorceress, Queen of the Berbers—Saidet, Queen of Persia
— Turkhan-Khatun, Sultana of Kharezmé — Hadee'yah a
Maiden who precedes the Bedouin Arabs in Battle.

THE ARABS, even in "the days of their
ignorance," were always a brave, warlike people. Their liberty, almost the
only wealth they possessed, was jealously
guarded with such courage and determination, that
the greatest nations of antiquity were unable to
subdue them. With the preaching of Mohammed
began the glorious days of Arabia. Their semi-
obscurity as a nation, hitherto, had been due solely
to the want of some common bond of union, some

link to bind together the princes of the various
tribes.   But when there was one leader to rally
round, one faith to propagate, one Paradise for those
who fell in conquering the heathen, the wild children
of the Desert proved that they could conquer foreign
countries as well as defend their native sands.
During the early days of Islamism, a vast number of
women, many belonging to the highest rank, followed
their relatives to battle, and fought for or against
the Koran as bravely as the men—nay, more than
once it was the valour of the Arab women that
retrieved the fortunes of the day.

The Prophet had many obstacles to overcome
before converting the great majority of his countrymen to the new faith.   Scarcely had he promulgated
his new doctrines, and gathered round him a few
faithful adherents, when  the  neighbouring chiefs
rose up, sword in hand, to stifle the new movement,
ere it attained more dangerous dimensions.  His
principal opponent during the first few years of the
Hegira was Abu Sofian, chief of the Koreishites,
who were, to a man, idolators.  The first military
exploit of the Islamites was despoiling a wealthy
caravan, led by that great chieftain, in the valley of
Bedar.  Abu Sofian, with three thousand soldiers,
avenged this insult on Mount Ohud, where the
Prophet, who had only nine hundred and fifty men,
was defeated and wounded; barely escaping with

his life. In this action, fought in the third year of
the Hegira (A.D. 611), Henda, the wife of Abu
Sofian, commanded the reserve of the Koreishites.
She was accompanied by fifteen other women, of
high rank. By exhortation and singing they
animated the men to fight well. Indeed, the
ultimate success of Abu Sofian was due, in a great
measure, to their presence.

Another of Mohammed's early opponents was
Forka, an Arab lady possessing a castle and immense
wealth. She was a kind of feudal peeress, and
retained a body of soldiers to defend her domain.
For some years she defied the Islamites; but at last
Zeid, one of the principal Moslem leaders, was
despatched to seize her castle. Forka defended herself
for some time with obstinacy and resolution; but,
after a troublesome and lengthy siege, the fortress
was taken by storm, and Forka was slain, together
with the best part of the garrison. Her daughter,
with all her wealth, became the prey of the victors.

The rapid success of Mohammed induced many
Arabs to take up the prophetic office on their own
account; imitators arose in various parts of Arabia,
sometimes achieving a temporary success almost
rivalling that of Mohammed. The most successful was named Mosseylemah, whose head-quarters
were the city and suburbs of Yemaumah. During
the life-time of Mohammed, little notice was taken

of this rival by the "true believers;" but after the
death of *the* Prophet, A.D. 632, the Caliph Abubeker
despatched Khaled, "the Sword of God," with a
large force to capture Yemaumah.  Mosseylemah
and nearly all his followers were slain in a fierce
action fought near the city.  Mujaia, one of the
impostor's principal officers, who had been made
prisoner before the battle, wishing to save his
fellow-citizens from total extermination, told Khaled
that the city was still crowded with brave warriors
ready to shed the last drop of blood in defence of
their homes; and he recommended the Arab general
to open negotiations at once.  Leaving the latter
to consider his advice, Mujaia found means to com-
municate with the inhabitants, whom he sent word
to arm all the women and girls in helmets and mail,
and to distribute them, armed with spears and
swords, on the walls.

Khaled perceiving the ramparts bristling with
arms, began to fear that an assault on a stronghold
so well defended might become an enterprise of some
magnitude.  So—though contrary to his pet 'war-
cry, "No quarter given, and none received,"—the
ruthless Islamite thought it best to accept a capitulation on comparatively mild terms.

On entering Yemaumah, Khaled soon saw the
deception practised upon him.  But, with a
generosity of which he was not often guilty, he

permitted the people to enjoy the benefits of the treaty.

During the siege of Damascus by Khaled, A.D. 633, several instances occurred of female heroism, both on the side of the Arabs and that of the Greeks. One day the governor of Damascus marched out to dislodge the besiegers; the latter, pretending to fly, led the Greeks to a considerable distance from the city. Then turning upon the foe, they assailed him on every side. Seffwaun the Salmian, a distinguished Moslem chief, seeing a Greek officer conspicuous for the splendour of his armour, knocked him down with a blow of his mace. He was about to strip the fallen chief, when he found himself fiercely attacked by the widow, who had accompanied her husband into battle, and whose death she now prepared to avenge. Seffwaun, wishing to avoid the dishonor of shedding the blood of a woman, contrived by dexterous manipulation of his sword to frighten his frail antagonist without wounding her or being himself wounded. She was soon compelled to retire for safety behind the swords and spears of her friends.

Another day some Arab women were captured by the Greeks during one of the skirmishes. While the Greeks were carousing in their tents, a girl named Khaullah, one of the prisoners, urged her sisters in captivity to arm themselves with tent-

poles, and brain anybody who approached them.
She set the example by shattering the skull of a
Greek soldier who was so imprudent as to venture
within reach of her arm.   A general conflict ensued ;
ending by Khaled and several Arab horsemen coming
to the rescue and carrying off the Islamite damsels.

Either this heroine, or another of the same name
afterwards turned the fortunes of the day in the
battle of Yermouks, which decided the fate of Syria.
The Arabs, far out-numbered by the Greeks, fled to
their tents, and refused to stir, despite the alternate
taunts or encouraging words of the women.   The
latter at last, in despair, armed themselves, and
withstood the foe till night closed in to end the
combat.   Next day, led by Khaullah, sister of one
of their principal commanders, the women again
marched to the attack.   In leading the van,
Khaullah was struck down by a Greek ; but Wafeira,
her principal female friend, ran to her aid and cut
off the soldier's head.   The Arabs, shamed into their
former courage by the noble conduct of the women,
attacked the Christians with such fury that the
latter were speedily routed, with a loss, it is said,
of one hundred and fifty thousand slain and about
fifty thousand made prisoners.

Khaullah, the leading heroine of this fight, was
afterwards married to the ill-starred Caliph Ali.

In the year 647, Abdallah, the Moslem governor

of Alexandria, crossed the Libyan Desert and appeared before the walls of Tripoli, at that time the most important city on the Coast of Barbary. After surprising and cutting to pieces several thousand Greeks who were marching to reinforce the garrison, the Arabs, frustrated in an attempt to storm the massive fortifications, prepared to lay formal siege. The city was strengthened very soon by Gregorius, the Greek prefect, who arrived at the head of one hundred and twenty thousand men. He rejected indignantly the option of the Koran or tribute. For several days both armies engaged in deadly combat, from dawn till the hour of noon, when, from fatigue and thirst caused by the blazing sun, they were compelled to seek shelter and refreshment.

The daughter of Gregorius, a young girl of great beauty, fought by her father's side throughout every engagement. She had been trained from early youth to excel in warlike exercises; and by the splendour of her arms and apparel she was conspicuous amidst the dust and confusion of the fight. Gregorius, to excite his soldiers to deeds of bravery, offered her hand and one hundred thousand pieces of gold to the man who brought him the head of Abdallah, the Moslem general. When the Arabs heard this they compelled their leader to withdraw from the field.

The Moslems, discouraged by the absence of their

chief, were rapidly giving way; but the counsels of
Zobeir, a brave Arab warrior, turned the fortunes
of the day.

"Retort on the infidels," cried he, "their un-
generous attempts. Proclaim throughout the ranks
that the head of Gregorius will be repaid with his
captive daughter, and the equal sum of one hundred
thousand pieces of gold."

This was accordingly proclaimed. At the same
time Zobeir resorted to a stratagem which took the
Greeks completely by surprise, and gained an easy
victory for the Arabs. The contending armies
having, as usual, separated after the engagement,
were retiring to their respective camps overcome by
fatigue, when the two Moslem chiefs, who had
placed themselves in ambush with fresh troops,
rushed out upon the exhausted Greeks and routed
them with fearful slaughter. The prefect himself was
slain by the hand of Zobeir; his daughter, while
seeking revenge or death in the thick of the fight,
was surrounded and captured.

Ayesha, daughter of Caliph Abubeker, was the
favourite wife of the Prophet. After the death of
her husband she lived in retirement, for twenty
years, at Medina. But she possessed a restless,
ambitious spirit, and had no inclination for a life of
repose and obscurity. After the sudden murder of

Caliph Othman, in 654, when Ali was elected, she refused to acknowledge the latter, and declared her belief that he had a share in the murder of his predecessor. The nation, divided into opposing factions, was soon plunged into civil war. The malcontents, headed by Ayesha, assembled in thousands at Mecca, and marched thence to Bassorah, where they expected to find warm support.

Arrived before Bassorah they were astounded to find the gates shut against them. Ayesha, mounted on a camel, advanced to the walls and harangued those assembled on the battlements. But she was old and crabbed, with sharp features and a shrill voice—rendered even more shrill by the rapidity with which she spoke,—so the people only laughed at her. The louder they laughed, the shriller her accents grew. They reproached her for riding forth, bare-faced, to foment dissension among the Faithful; and they jeered at her followers for bringing their old grandmother in place of their young and handsome wives.

However, a number of the citizens were secretly in favour of the malcontents; and the friends of Ayesha seized the palace one dark night, bastinadoed the governor, plucked out his beard, and sent him back to his master. Great, however, was the dismay of Ayesha when the Caliph encamped one morning before Bassorah; but, resolved not to give

6—2

way, she rejected the proposals of Ali, and plunged
both armies into a fierce engagement before very
well knowing what she was about. But terrified
at the horrors of war, to which until this day she
was almost a stranger, the old woman besought
Kaub, who led her camel, to throw himself between
the combatants. In trying to obey her command
he was slain.

The large white camel of Ayesha soon became
the rallying-point of the insurgents, around which
the fury of the battle concentrated. The reins
were held alternately by the Modian Arabs, who
chanted pieces of poetry; and it is said that out of
the tribe of Benni Beiauziah alone not less than
*two hundred and eighty* lost a hand on this occasion.
The howdah, pierced all over with arrows, had
something the appearance of a porcupine or a giant
pincushion.

After the battle had raged for several hours, the
Caliph, seeing plainly that it would go on so long
as the camel remained alive, ordered his chiefs to
direct all their efforts towards cutting down the
beast. First one leg was cut off; but the camel
maintained its erect position. Another leg was cut
off; yet the animal remained immovable. For a
moment the soldiers of Ali thought the camel
was a sorcerer or a genie. But a third leg was cut
off, and the camel sank to the ground.

The battle soon ended ; all resistance ceased when the insurgents knew that their leader was taken. Ali treated his prisoner with that true chivalry which had already sprung up amongst the Arabs. He sent her home to Medina, escorted by female attendants disguised as soldiers, and while he lived she was not permitted to meddle in politics. After the murder of Ali she resumed her former position. Many years after, when Moawyah wished to make the Caliphate hereditary in his family, he purchased the influence of Ayesha by the gift of a pair of bracelets valued at one hundred and fifty thousand dinars, or nearly seventy thousand pounds.

The "Battle of the Camel," as it is generally styled by Oriental historians, was fought in December, A.D. 656, (A.H. 36.)

During the reign of Caliph Abdul - Malek the Islamites in northern Africa found a most formidable opponent in Cahina the sorceress, Queen of the Berbers. Under the lead of this pseudo-prophetess, the original natives of Barbary made a determined stand for many years against the Koran.

Cahina directed her followers to lay waste the lands that lay between Egypt and her dominions, telling them that it was the fruitfulness of those districts which caused the Arab invasions. Her commands were only too faithfully executed.

Cities, towns, and villages were destroyed; fields
desolated, trees cut down, and the entire face of the
land changed from a beautiful garden planted with
waving palms and lovely flowers, into an arid waste
with scarcely a tree or blade of grass to be seen.

But this scheme ultimately proved the ruin of
Cahina. The natives of the ruined districts joyfully
welcomed the Moslems on their next invasion. Cahina again took the field with all her forces; but her
ranks this time were thinned by desertion. She
was speedily defeated and made prisoner with her
principal advisers. Rejecting the proposals of the
Arab general—the Koran or tribute—her head was
cut off, put in a camphor-scented casket of great
price, and sent to the Caliph.

Although Persia was one of the earliest conquests
effected by the followers of Islam, scarcely two
centuries had elapsed before it was divided into a
number of independent states, ruled by Arab,
Turkish, or Persian princes. Towards the close of the
tenth century, Queen Seidet, widow of one of these
independent monarchs, governed the state as regent
for her son, who was a minor. She ruled with so
much wisdom, and under her guidance the kingdom
flourished so greatly, that she had every reason to
be offended when her son, grown old enough to take
the reins of government, appointed Avicenna, the

family physician, to be his Grand Vizier, and committed everything into his hands. Avicenna treated the queen with so little respect that the latter retired from court, raised troops, and marched against her son, whose forces she easily routed. Not wishing, however, to deprive him of the throne, she merely acted as his chief adviser, and aided him with salutary counsels so long as she lived.

Sultan Mahmoud, founder of the Gaznevide dynasty, held Seidet in the deepest respect. While she lived he refrained from attacking her son's dominions; but after her death he annexed them without scruple.

In these days few persons, save students of Oriental history, have even so much as heard of Kharezmé, in Tartary; yet in the eleventh and twelfth centuries it was considered by surrounding nations as the most powerful state in Asia, and its court the most magnificent. At the beginning of the thirteenth century, it was actually, although not nominally, governed by Turkhan Khatun, mother of the reigning Sultan. In those days the Mongols, under the irresistible Jenghiz Khan, were advancing with rapid strides towards Europe. It was not long before they besieged the capital of Kharezmé. The city held out for twelve months against the Mongol hordes commanded by the three sons of Jenghiz

Khan.  The inhabitants, male and female, made a
defence worthy of their ancient fame.  Even the
women aided in the numberless sorties made from
the city.  But at last, despite their bravery, the
place was taken by storm.  Men and women alike
fought hand to hand with the Mongols, and retired
from street to street, till scarcely any remained
alive.

According to the lowest computation more than
one hundred thousand Kharezmians were slain
during the siege.  The valour displayed by the women
became so famous throughout Asia, that many
Oriental historians, by way of accounting for it,
gravely assert that the people of Kharezmó were
descended from the Amazons.

Mr. Palgrave, who travelled through Arabia in
1862-3, says that it is customary amongst the
Bedouin Arabs, when they go into battle, to have
their army preceded by a maiden of good family,
styled a Hadee'yah, who rides on a camel into the
midst of the fight, encouraging the men to fight
bravely by reciting pieces of extempore poetry,
satirical or heroic, as best suits the occasion.  Very
frequently the Hadee'yah is slain.  Such was the
fate of a brave girl, noted for her eloquence and
gigantic stature, who led on the Amjan Bedouins at
Koweyt rather more than twenty years ago, against

Abd-Allah, heir to the throne of Nejed. This "Arabian Bellona" was slain by the lance of a Nejdean warrior, and her death is said to have been the principal cause of the final rout of the Amjan army.

## V.

EUROPE, during the two or three centuries
after the downfall of the Roman Empire,
bears a strong resemblance to Greece
during the heroic age. In the Nibelun-
gen, the Iliad of those days, we read of godlike
heroes, Herculean warriors, giant princes, and Amazon
queens. That was an age when might constituted
right, when rulers led their own armies in the field,
where the lead was given to the strongest or the
most daring.

The Salique law seems in those days to have been
very generally disregarded—if indeed it had been

introduced as yet; for we read of more than one
queen who ruled alone over the more or less barbarous kingdoms of Europe. Æneas Sylvius narrates
how a warlike queen named Libyssa ascended the
throne of Bohemia on the death of her father, King
Crocus. Her husband, Przemislas, whom she espoused in 632, being originally only a peasant, was
probably a humble, weak-minded individual, ruled
by his wife; for the queen proceeded to enrol the
greater number of her female subjects into a species
of militia. They were trained, like the Amazons,
to the use of arms and to ride on horseback. After
the death of Libyssa, the narrator further says that
the principal favourite of the queen, Valasca, with
the assistance of the female troops, seized the throne,
and held it until her death, which occurred seven
years later. Resolved to form a nation of Amazons,
Valasca passed a law that all male children should
have their right eyes put out and their thumbs cut
off, to keep them from using bow and arrows. And
this barbarous order was rigorously enforced while
Valasca lived, the men not daring to raise any
complaint. The demise of this Amazon-queen soon
restored everything to its natural order.

Wanda, the first Queen-Regnant of Poland, was
unanimously elected by the people on the death of
her father, Cracus, about the year 700. She was a

talented woman, and esteemed herself fully capable of conducting the government without the assistance of a husband. To the numerous offers of marriage she received, a refusal was the invariable answer. At last Rudiger, a German prince, hoping to bring about a happy union by force of arms, invaded Poland with a great army.

Wanda raised troops, and advanced to meet the invaders. When the opposing armies came in sight, Rudiger, believing that his warlike preparations must needs have terrified the queen, besought her to accept him, and thus save the lives of their soldiers. Wanda answered that no man should ever share her throne, because he would love her kingdom better than herself. When this spirited answer was spread amongst Rudiger's officers, they refused to fight against so heroic a queen. Surrounding the prince, they endeavoured to dissuade him from risking a battle; but finding their remonstrances vain, they refused to second his efforts, and Rudiger, in despair, flung himself on his sword.

Wanda returned in triumph to Cracow. She never received another proposal of marriage.

In the year 711 the Moors, commanded by Tarik, crossed the Straits of Gibraltar and invaded Spain. Even after the defeat and death of their king, the Goths disputed every foot of ground before giving

way to the Infidels. The latter, impeded at every
step, were glad to grant peace on almost any terms.
One of the principal Gothic leaders was Theodomir,
or Tudmir Ben Gobdas, a Spanish noble belonging
to one of the most honourable families in the land.
He possessed large estates in the South, and his
authority over them was so great that not only was
the district named after him, the Land of Tudmir,
but he was styled King. Having been totally routed
in a battle, when the greater number of his soldiers
were slain, he escaped to the fortified citadel of
Tudmir, where he was soon besieged by the Moors.

Finding his position grow daily more and more
untenable, Theodomir resorted to an expedient,
already practised by the people of Yemaumah when
besieged by Khaled. He commanded all the women
to put on male attire, to tie their hair under
their chin (to imitate long beards), and to appear,
armed with bows and arrows, lances, swords, and
shields, on the towers and battlements, in sight of
the Moors. He himself, with his few remaining
soldiers, stood in front, to conceal as much as
possible these feminine guards.

The Moors, overrating the strength of the garrison,
offered Theodomir advantageous terms, which he
accepted. Although they afterwards discovered the
fraud, the Infidels scrupulously observed the treaty.

The women of Tortosa distinguished themselves

so highly in some skirmishes with the Moors, that
a military Order of Knighthood was conferred upon
them.

The word "Infantry" is said to owe its origin to
one of the Spanish Infantas, who, hearing that her
father had been defeated by the Moors, raised a body
of foot-soldiers, and placing herself at their head,
defeated the infidels. In memory of her bravery,
foot-soldiers were henceforth styled Infantry.

The Moors never could obtain a footing north of
the Pyrenees; yet, despite the invariable want of
success attending their attempts, they made constant
incursions into France, besieging towns, burning
villages, and ravaging the open country. Amongst
other cities besieged by them was Carcassonne,
situated on the banks of the river Aude, governed
in those days by queen Carcas, famous for her
military prowess. When Charlemagne, a few years
previously, besieged the city, it was defended so
courageously that he permitted the queen to retain
the sovereignty.

The Saracens, ridiculing the notion of a female
warrior, declared that, in place of fighting, she ought
to be spinning. This contemptuous speech, spoken
immediately under the city walls, was overheard by
queen Carcas. Arming herself with a lance, to
which, as if it had been a distaff, she attached a

quantity of hemp, she set the hemp on fire, and rushed into the midst of the Saracens, who fled, terrified, in all directions.

The shield and lance of queen Carcas may yet be seen at Carcassonne. Over the city gate there is an effigy of the royal heroine, with the inscription " Carcas sum."

While the South of Europe was overrun by the Saracens, England, Ireland, and Scotland were harassed by the terrible Danes, who for several centuries kept these islands in constant terror. The most powerful opponent of the Danes in England was, as everyone knows, King Alfred the Great. During the latter years of his reign, the land was tolerably secure from invasion; but after his death the Vikings and their wild followers came swarming over the country again, burning, plundering, massacreing, just as they had done before Alfred drove them away. Elfrida, the eldest daughter of King Alfred, inherited all her father's courage and warlike spirit, and, like him, proved an implacable foe to the Danes. She was married early to Ethelred, Earl of Mercia; and on his death the government of the province devolved upon the widow. And nobly did she fulfil her trust. Mercia was greatly harassed by the Danes—as, indeed, was the entire country in those days. The Welsh joined in alliance

with the invaders, and would have marched to their
aid but for the promptitude of Elfrida, who entered
Wales, 916, at the head of an army, and took Breck-
nock by storm, capturing therein Queen Anghared
and many of her attendants. The "Lady of Mercia"
had another motive in this invasion, which rendered
Wales tributary to the Saxons; and this motive was
the desire to avenge the death of the good Abbot
Egbert, whom the Welsh had slain.

King Owen fled to Derby, where he was kindly
received by the Danes. When Elfrida learned this
she marched thither, and captured the city " before
Lammas," 918. So reckless was she of her own
safety on this memorable day, that it had almost
proved to be her last. Pressing at the head of her
troops through the narrow gateway where a vast
multitude of Danes barred the way, many of her
principal officers were struck down, and four of her
guards were slain by the hand of the Welsh king.
Gwynne, lord of Ely, and steward of Elfrida, perceiving the danger of the princess, set the gates on
fire, and rushed furiously upon the Welsh and Danes,
who gave way before his onslaught.

Owen, unable to escape, preferred to fall by
his own hand than yield himself prisoner to a
woman.

Two years later, in 920, Efrilda recaptured Leicester and York from the Danes; and besides

repairing the fortifications of the former city, encompassed it with a massive wall of such strength that Matthew Paris styles it *indissoluble.*

Shortly after this, and before the war was over, Elfleda died at Tamworth, in Staffordshire, leaving an unmarried daughter named Elswina. She was buried at Gloucester, in the porch of St. Peter's monastery, a building erected at her own expense.

This heroine has been praised by all the old historians for her prudence, courage, and talent for governing. Ingulphus says that considering the great actions of her life, the cities she built, the castles she fortified, and the armies she raised, Elfleda "might have been thought a man." She was generally styled queen by the Mercians, who regarded themselves as her subjects.

According to tradition it was the same wild Vikings, the terror of our land, who founded the mighty Russian empire; and their successors, the Grand Dukes and Czars, have ever since retained that thirst for conquest which distinguished the roving Normans. The Grand Duke Igor was one of the first among the successors of Rurik who caused the Russian standard to be feared by surrounding states. After subduing most of the neighbouring towns, his victorious career was suddenly brought to a close in 945, during an expedition against the Drevlians, by whom he was surrounded, and put to the sword with all his troops.

Igor was succeeded by his son Sviatoslaf, the first Christian sovereign of Russia. The prince being too young to conduct the government, his mother, Olga, undertook the regency. The Drevlians, fancying the royal widow would be easily intimidated, sent to demand her in marriage for their prince. But Olga, after causing their ambassadors to be slain (by various quaint stratagems which Nestor has preserved) called out her troops, placed herself at their head, and marched against the Drevlians, taking her son with her to teach him the art of war. After destroying all the towns and villages of the enemy, she laid siege to Karosten, their capital, which was built entirely of wood—the very name signifying "wall of bark." Finding the city too strong and too well defended, she made proposals of peace to the inhabitants, declaring that she would be satisfied with three sparrows and a pigeon from each house, as tribute. The people joyfully complied, and sent the birds to the Russian camp. Olga caused the birds to be let loose, with lighted torches tied to their tails; they, of course, flew back to their nests in the house-eaves of Karosten. The town was soon in a blaze from end to end. The terrified inhabitants, flying to escape the flames, were met by the swords and lances of the Russians. The

Drevlian prince and his court perished in the massacre, as indeed, did nearly every one in the city,
save the dregs of the population.

Having glutted her thirst for revenge, Olga
made a progress through Russia, taking Sviatoslaf
with her. Towns and villages arose at her command,
taxation was regulated on a better footing; and by
various measures highly beneficial to the prosperity
of the country, the Grand Duchess proved herself a most able ruler. In 955 she went to Constantinople to be baptised a Christian, and in the
course of a few years the Greek faith spread
through the land, and paganism was abolished.

When Sviatoslaf grew old enough to rule his
own dominions, Olga resigned the reins of government. She lived in retirement for several years,
and died in 968 at an advanced age.

In the Middle Ages, chemistry and mathematics
were things known to few people except the monks;
any man who studied the sciences was styled an
alchemist, and suspected of being in league with
the Evil One. When it was a woman who gave
herself up to learned studies, the people could
scarcely be withheld from tearing "the sorceress"
to pieces. Occasionally, however, despite what
the world said, noble ladies, especially on the
Continent, did apply their minds to what in those

7—2

days went by the name of the Black Art. Amongst
these was Richilda, Countess of Hainault, who
married Baldwin the Good, eldest son of Baldwin,
Marquis of Flanders, one of whose daughters,
Matilda, became the wife of William the Conqueror,
and another of Tosti Godwinsson, son of the powerful
Earl Godwin.  The fame of Richilda as a wicked
sorceress caused her to be anything but a favourite
in the country; and when her husband died, Robert
le Frison, Count of Friesland, and brother of the
deceased, endeavoured to wrest Flanders from her
young son Arnulf, or Arnoul, who was little more
than a boy.  William the Conqueror espoused the
cause of Richilda, and sent over Fitz-Osbern, Earl of
Hereford, the tyrant of the Welsh, to her aid.  The
Countess also implored the assistance of her liege
lord, the king of France.

A battle took place on St. Peter's Day, 1071, at
Bavinchorum, near Cassel; Richilda and Fitz-
Osbern commanded their troops in person.  The
left wing of the foe was routed, and Robert le Frison
made prisoner and sent to St. Omer.  But this
success was counterbalanced by the death of Fitz-
Osbern and young Arnoul.  Richilda's forces fled
in confusion, and the heroine was made prisoner.

An exchange was effected, by which Richilda and
the Frison regained their liberty.  The countess
immediately set about raising fresh troops to avenge

the death of her boy. The contending armies met again ; this time at Broqueroi, near Mons, where the troops of Richilda were routed with so terrible a slaughter that the scene of the conflict was afterwards known under the name of "the Hedges of Death." All hope now fled the breast of Richilda. Escaping from the field, she took refuge in a convent, where the rest of her days were passed under the severest penances—to atone, as folks said, for her past dealings with the Prince of Darkness.

## VI.

T would be difficult at the present day to appreciate the wild enthusiasm spread throughout Europe by the preaching of Peter the Hermit. Thousands from all classes—kings, princes, nobles, priests, peasants, beggars, all alike impelled by the same blind impulse, many amongst them scarcely knowing where they were going or for what they went to fight,—hastened to take up arms against the Infidel.

The enthusiasm was not, as it would probably in our days, confined to one, nor even to three or four nations. " There were men," says Robert of Gloucester :—

> " Of Normandy, of Denmark, of Norway, of Bretagne,
> Of Wales, and of Ireland, of Gascony, of Spain,
> Of Provence, of Saxony, and of Allemayne,
> Of Scotland, and of Greece, of Rome and Aquitaine."

Ay, and women too. The first Crusading armies which set out in the spring of 1096, commanded by Peter the Hermit, Gaultier-sans-Avoir, and other leaders of less reputation, comprised nearly as many women as men. Even where they did not contend hand to hand with the Saracens, these heroines cheered the warriors by marching with them in the ranks, by carrying food and ammunition to the battlefield, by speaking with enthusiasm of the cause for which they had armed. It was, indeed, owing as much to the courage and endurance of the women, who suffered without a murmur the miseries of cold, hunger, and want of clothing, as to their own indomitable bravery that the Templars owed the capture of Antioch. William of Tyre, speaking of the grand review held before Nice in 1099, says that exclusive of the cavalry, who, to the number of one hundred thousand were well armed in helmets and mail, there were found six hundred thousand Crusaders of both sexes, many of them little children.

When the second Crusade was preached, many
ladies, especially in France and Germany, formed
themselves into squadrons and regiments of Amazons,
and assumed the arms and armour of the Templars.
The commander of the German Amazons, who, says
Michaud, was more admired for her dress than her
courage, received the title of the " Golden Footed
Dame," or the " Lady with the Golden Legs," on
account of her magnificent gilded buskins and spurs.
She enrolled her troop under the banner of the
emperor Conrad, who started for the East 1147.
The French Amazons were commanded by their
queen, Eleonora of Aquitaine (afterwards wife of
Henry II. of England). Forming themselves into
a squadron of light cavalry, they went through a
regular course of military training, and, by constant
exercise, they acquired tolerable proficiency in the
use of arms.

Mezerai, speaking of these " squadrons of females,"
declares that by their valour they " rendered credible
all that has been said of the prowess of the Amazons ;"
but, certes, those who followed King Louis to the
Holy Land rendered themselves more notable for
rashness and folly than manly courage. They set
out in the year 1147, with the bold determination to
share all the fatigues and brave all the dangers
incident to a crusade ; but their first essay in the
presence of the enemy proved sufficient to put an

end to their gallant resolutions and cover their leader with ridicule. The corps of Amazons, escorted by a band of sterner warriors commanded by a distinguished knight, had been sent on in advance, with strict orders from the king to encamp on the heights of Laodicea, and there await his arrival. They reached the spot as the sun was setting, and the black, dreary rocks appeared to the romantic, but inexperienced eye of Eleonora, an exceedingly uninviting situation for a resting place. With the haughty imperiousness of her nature, she insisted on turning aside to a beautiful valley watered by cool streams, and overshadowed by lofty palms, where, despite the warnings and expostulations of the brave captain who led her escort, she encamped.

In this charming but unprotected dale they were soon attacked by a party of Saracens. King Louis arrived barely in time to save the corps of Amazons from capture. Compelled to hazard an engagement under peculiarly disadvantageous circumstances against an enemy who received reinforcements from moment to moment, Louis was so near being made prisoner as to be obliged to seek refuge in a tree. The Christians were victorious, but it was with heavy losses. Eleonora and her followers retired to the court of her cousin Raymond, Prince of Antioch, and there passed the rest of the season.

While the Crusades lasted, ladies continued to

accompany husbands and lovers to the East.   In the arsenal of the palace at Genoa there are, or were some few years since, several light cuirasses, made for a band of Genoese ladies, who, towards the close of the thirteenth century, wished to join in a crusade against the Turks.   However, by the entreaties of Pope Boniface VIII., who wrote an autograph letter for the purpose, they were persuaded to relinquish their design.

Pierre Gentien, an old French poet, who flourished at the latter end of the thirteenth century, has left a species of epic in rhyme, wherein he describes a tournament held by certain noble dames who were about departing with the knights beyond the seas. In this poem the author, describing how the combatants, to acquire proficiency in the use of arms, disputed the prize of valour with all the courage and enthusiasm of the knights of those days, takes the opportunity to name forty or fifty, the most beautiful ladies of their time.   His poem has been therefore admired rather as being a memoir of the old French families than for the excellence of the poetry.

The somewhat ridiculous termination to her first essay in presence of the foe did not entirely quench the military ardour of Eleonora of Aquitaine.   After she had been for some years the wife of king Henry

II., she stirred up her sons, Richard and John, to rebellion against their father ; and went so far as to appear in masculine attire, at the head of their forces in Aquitaine. And thus clad, she was made prisoner.

When Prince Arthur was prosecuting his claims on the English crown, Philip Augustus, the French king, sent him with a military retinue into Normandy, then in the hands of the English. The French barons laid siege to Mirebeau, a fortified town near Poitiers. It was defended for King John by Eleonora, who, though she had then attained the age of fourscore, was as active as ever, and had only just returned from a journey into Spain—a matter of some difficulty in those days. When the French had captured the town, the veteran Amazon threw herself into a strong tower which served as a sort of citadel ; and here she held out bravely till the arrival of John with reinforcements, on the night between July 31st and August 1, 1202 ; when the besiegers were compelled to surrender.

During the wars between the Empress Maud and Stephen, the latter was ably seconded by his queen, Matilda of Boulogne. For the first five years of his usurpation, the king was disturbed only by the revolt of Baldwin, Earl of Exeter, and the invasion of David, King of Scotland. Matilda showed herself to

be an able politician and a brave soldier. In June,
1137, she laid siege to Dover Castle, which had been
seized by the rebels, and, at the same time, sent
orders to her Boulogne subjects to blockade the fortress by sea.

In July, 1139, the empress, escorted by her brother
Robert, Earl of Gloucester, landed in England.
After several battles, of which little is known, she
defeated and captured King Stephen near Lincoln,
1141. The empress was at once proclaimed queen
of England, and after sending Stephen in irons to
Bristol, she entered London. Matilda made humble
suit for the liberty of her lord, and offered, in his
name, to resign all claim to the crown; but the
empress refused, save on the petitioner also surrendering her inheritance of Boulogne. The queen
refused; and with the assistance of William of
Ypres, Stephen's talented but unpopular minister,
she raised the standard of the king in Surrey and
Kent, where a large party were in favour of the royal
captive.

"In the pages of superficially-written histories,"
remarks Miss Strickland, "much is said of the
prowess and military skill displayed by Prince
Eustace at this period; but Eustace was scarcely
seven years old at the time when these efforts were
made for the deliverance of his royal sire; therefore
it is plain to those who reflect on the evidence of

dates, that it was the high-minded and prudent queen, his mother, who avoided all Amazonian display by acting under the name of her son."

The empress, being warned that the Londoners, weary of her insolence, had a mind to serve her as she had served Stephen, fled from the city by night, and laid siege to Winchester Castle. The men of London and Kent, headed by Matilda, Eustace, and William of Ypres, were soon at the city gates, and Maud was closely invested for several days in her palace. To escape the horrors of a city in flames, the empress feigned herself dead, and her body was conveyed to Gloucester. Robert, her brother, was made prisoner, and his liberty was purchased by the release of Stephen.

From this time the fortunes of the empress rapidly declined. She was so closely invested in Oxford during the inclement weather of 1142, that she was compelled to dress herself and her attendants in white, which, as the ground was covered with snow, more readily escaped observation, and so steal away from the town. The war continued to rage with the utmost fury for the next five years; but Maud, weary at last of the miserable struggle, returned to Normandy in 1147.

Queen Matilda died at Henningham Castle, in Essex, on May 3rd, 1151, a little more than three years before her husband. The empress out-

Good in 1189 ; but the throne was usurped by Tancred, her natural brother.  Henry invaded the Neapolitan states in 1191 ; but though successful at first, a terrible mortality in his camp compelled him to raise the siege of Naples and retire from the country.

After the death of Tancred, his widow resigned all claim to the crown ; stipulating that her infant son, William, should be left in possession of Tarentum. But the cruel and perfidious emperor, who had failed in all his attempts on Naples and Sicily during the life-time of the king, cast the boy into prison, after putting out his eyes, imprisoned the queen and the princesses in a convent, and carried the royal treasures to Germany.

When the emperor returned to his own land, Naples and Sicily rose against his tyranny.  Hastening back with a mighty army, Henry defeated the rebels, and commanded that the leaders should suffer the most excruciating tortures.  Constantia, shocked at his barbarity, quarrelled with her husband, cast off her allegiance, and stirred up the Sicilians to a fresh rebellion.  Thousands flocked to her standard, and the empress, at this time fifty years old, led them against the German troops.  Henry, who had sent away most of his soldiers to the Holy Land, was defeated, and compelled to submit to the terms dictated by Constantia.

The emperor died at Messina in 1197, shortly after the conclusion of the treaty, and his wife has been accused of administering poison, to rid her people of a cruel and vindictive tyrant. After his death, Constantia lived peacefully in Sicily as regent of the island and guardian of her infant son, the Emperor Frederick II. She died three years later, in the year 1200.

Returning to England, we find Dame Nichola de Camville, a noted heroine of those days, personally engaged on the royal side during the Barons' wars. Nichola de Hara, widow of Gerard, Lord Camville was co-sheriff for the county of Lincolnshire. She held the Castle of Lincoln for King John against Gilbert de Gaunt, who had captured the city; and after the death of John she defended it for his son, Henry III. Shortly after the death of King John, the Count de la Perche, a French knight commanding the Confederate Barons, marched to Lincoln at the head of six hundred knights and twenty thousand soldiers, and besieged the castle. It was defended by Dame Nichola till the arrival of the Earl of Pembroke in May, 1217, when the battle, afterwards known as "Lincoln Fair," quelled for a time the rebellion of the English barons, and established Henry III. on the throne.

Turn which way we will, we see nothing but civil wars and struggles for supremacy between crowned heads and nobles. Crossing to France, some nine or ten years later, we find the great vassals of the throne conspiring to deprive Queen Blanche of the regency. However, Blanche of Castille was not a woman easily intimidated. At the head of a large army, she went with the young king (her son) to Brittany, the seat of the conspiracy. The malcontent nobles, not being prepared to meet the royal forces in the field, submitted for a time.

In the following year, 1227, the royal troops defeated and captured Raymond, Count of Toulouse, leader of the Albigeois, and the queen treated her noble captive so harshly that the French lords again took up arms, led by the Duke of Brittany. Despite the severity of the winter, the queen-regent and her son marched into Brittany; and after surmounting terrible obstacles from the cold, and from the snow and ice, which stopped both roads and rivers, laid siege to the stronghold of Bellesme. This fortress which from the thickness of its walls, was supposed to be impregnable, had a garrison of Bretons, supported by a body of English auxiliaries. The besieged were in hopes that the royal army, horribly decimated by the severe weather, would be compelled soon to retire. But the queen was not the one to yield when she had once resolved on anything. To preserve her soldiers, hundreds of whom perished from the bitter cold, she caused immense fires to be kept constantly blazing, and offered high rewards to all who brought wood into camp. To encourage the men she slept in the open air by the bivouac fires, conversed with the troops, and encouraged officers and privates alike by her affability and con-descension.

Queen Blanche pressed the siege with unyielding determination. After two assaults had been made the great tower was dismantled, and the garrison surrendered. The Duke of Brittany was made prisoner, though, through motives of policy, he was speedily set at liberty. The queen next took Nantes and Acenis; and the revolt was brought to a close in 1230 by the surrender of the Count de Marche.

From the courage and military tact displayed by the queen during the siege of Bellesmes, she received the complimentary title of "the Great Captain."

The regency of Blanche ended in 1235, and Louis IX. took the government into his own hands; but she again took up the regency in 1248, when her son set forth on his crusade. She died in 1252, before St. Louis came home from his ill-starred expedition.

So deep was the respect entertained for the

memory of Blanche of Castille, that many of the queen-dowagers of France assumed the surname of Blanche, as the Roman emperors took the title of Augustus.

Until the thirteenth century, Prussia was inhabited by heathen barbarians. In 1226, Conrad of Masovia gave the Teutonic Knights a strip of land on the Vistula, that they might protect Poland from the Prussian savages. For more than half a century the knights carried on a war of extermination against the natives; again and again were the Prussian tribes vanquished, again and again they rebelled. In 1240 a general insurrection of greater magnitude burst forth, and nearly all the knights were massacred. Those who escaped—principally the Knights of the Cross—took refuge in the castles of Thorn, Reden, and Culm, where they were soon beleaguered by the Prussians. The knights in Culm were induced by a stratagem to come out, when they fell into an ambuscade, and were all slain. The city would have fallen had not the women closed the gates, clad themselves in mail, and mounted the walls with spears in their hands. The Prussians, deceived by this stratagem, withdrew their forces, believing that Culm was still strongly garrisoned by sturdy knights.

Prussia was at last converted to Christianity, and adopted the manners and customs of Germany, of which it is now the leading State.

The contests between the Guelfs and Ghibelines proved fatal to Italian liberty. Might became right, tyrants arose on every side, and either by open force or by fraud, possessed themselves of the sovereign power in some one of the Lombardian cities and the adjacent territories. The various military leaders, whether Italians or Germans, were mere freebooters, accountable to no one for their acts, permitting the utmost license to themselves and their followers. One of the most infamous of these mercenaries was Acciolin, who was not a brutal and rapacious robber, but a man of refined cruelty. His favourite mode of torture was to fasten his prisoners to half-putrified corpses, and leave the living and the dead to rot away together.

In 1253, this fiend in human shape captured Bassano by storm, after a tiresome siege. The garrison was commanded by John Baptista de Porta, who was either governor or lord of the place. Blanche de Rossi, his wife, a native of Padua, put on armour, mounted the ramparts, and fought by the side of her husband. When the town fell the governor was slain, and Blanche, after making a desperate resistance, was made prisoner and led in triumph before Acciolin. Directly the villain set eyes upon his beautiful captive, he was seized with a violent passion for her; and to escape him, she sprang, clad as she was in armour, through a window. But in place of death, she only met with a sprained shoulder. Directly she recovered from her swoon the tyrant sent for her again, and finding his renewed protestations were repulsed with loathing, he obtained by force what was denied to his prayers. Blanche then withdrew to the place where her husband's body had been thrown, and flinging herself into the open grave, was crushed to death by the falling earth and stones.

In the year 1333, King Edward III., espousing the cause of Edward Baliol, invaded Scotland. The battle of Hallidon Hill, July 29th, in which the Regent Douglas was defeated, placed Baliol on the throne; and Edward, carried away by his ambitious designs upon the French throne, left his army in charge of the Earls of Arundel and Salisbury, and returned to England. Montague, Earl of Salisbury, laid siege to the castle of Dunbar, a place of great importance, esteemed as the key of Scotland, on the south-east border. It had been fortified very recently; and in the absence of the Earl of March, was defended by the countess, who, from the dark colour of her complexion, was popularly styled "Black Agnes." She was the daughter of Randolph, Earl of Moray, and inherited from her father a fierce, intrepid spirit. During the five months' siege she performed all the duties of a bold and skilful commander, and the garrison had the utmost confidence in her abilities. Constantly on the ramparts, she derided the English with biting sarcasms. When the battering-engines hurled stones against the walls, she scornfully told one of her female attendants to wipe off the dust with her handkerchief.

The Earl of Salisbury knew well the kind of foe he had to deal with. One day he was superintend-ing the siege operations, when an arrow from the castle whizzed past and struck a knight who stood by, piercing through his chain-mail haubergeon, and killing him on the spot.

"There comes one of my lady's tire-pins," exclaimed the Earl. "Agnes's love-shafts go straight to the heart!"

A monster called the "sow," a huge engine covered with hides, somewhat resembling the testudo of the Romans, was at last rolled to the foot of the walls. When the countess saw this ponderous machine coming, she cried in a loud, mocking voice :—

"Montague, beware! your sow shall soon cast her pigs!"

She quickly verified her words by hurling an immense piece of rock upon the "sow," crushing both it and its occupants to pieces.

Salisbury finding he could not succeed by fair means, bribed the gate-keeper to leave the gates

open on the following night. The porter disclosed
this to the countess, who directed him to keep to his
bargain and say nothing about it. The Earl, who
commanded the party that were to seize the castle,
rode through the darkness at the head of his soldiers,
found the gates open according to agreement, and
was about to enter, when one of his men, John
Copeland, passed in front of him. The portcullis
was suddenly dropped; Copeland, mistaken for his
master, remained a prisoner. The Earl was saved
by his men, who dragged him back just in time.
Agnes, from a high turret, saw that the general had
escaped.

"Farewell, Montague!" she cried. "I intended
that you should have supped with us to-night, and
assisted in defending the fortress against the
English."

Salisbury, despairing of being able to take the
place, either by treachery or by storm, turned the
siege into a blockade, closely investing the castle by
sea and land, and tried to starve the garrison out
into a surrender. Alexander Ramsay, hearing of
the extremities to which Black Agnes was reduced,
embarked with a party of forty resolute men, eluded
the vigilance of the English, and entered the castle,
under cover of night, by a postern next the sea.
Sallying out again, they attacked and dispersed the
advanced guard of the besiegers. Salisbury, dis-

heartened by so many reverses, withdrew his forces, after having remained before Dunbar for nineteen weeks.

About this time the duchy of Brittany was the subject of contention between two rivals, John, Count de Montfort, son of the late duke, and Charles of Blois, who had married the duke's grand-daughter. Philip de Valois, King of France, decided the dispute in favour of Charles, and despatched a large army to establish him in the capital. Edward III., of England, at once declared for the Count de Montfort, as an enemy to the house of Valois, which he—King Edward—wished to drive from the throne of France.

The count was betrayed into the hands of his rival by some malcontent nobles. But Jane, the brave countess, sustained his sinking fortunes "with the courage of a man and the heart of a lion." Directly the news of her husband's capture arrived at Rennes, where she resided, the countess assembled the citizens, showed them her infant son, and entreated them not to desert the last male heir of their ancient dukes. Her eloquence, beauty, and courage produced a magical effect. The people swore to defend her and her son to the last extremity.

The countess next visited all the strongholds throughout Brittany, and excited the people to resist

the French, and to adopt the requisite measures of
defence. Then, sending her boy to England, she
shut herself up in Hennebonne, and there awaited
the reinforcements promised by King Edward.

Charles of Blois entered Brittany, captured
Rennes, and despatched a force, commanded by
Prince Louis of Spain, to besiege Hennebonne.
The garrison, animated by the presence of the
valiant countess, made a resolute defence. Jane
herself performed prodigies of valour. Clad in
armour from head to foot, she stood foremost in the
breach, sustaining every attack of the foe with the
utmost *sang froid*, or ran from post to post, according
as the troops required encouragement or reinforce-
ment.

One day the besiegers, engaged in an attack on
the town, left their camp totally unprotected. The
countess, perceiving their neglect, sallied forth by a
postern-gate at the head of five hundred picked
men, set fire to the enemy's baggage and magazines,
and created such universal alarm that the besiegers
gave over their assault on the town to intercept her
return. Jane, seeing that her retreat was cut off
that way, galloped towards Arrai, where she arrived
in safety. In five days she returned, cut her way
through the camp of Charles, and re-entered the
town. By this time, however, the breaches in the
walls had grown so numerous that the place was

deemed untenable. The bishop of Léon, despite the entreaties, the prayers of Jane, resolved to capitulate, and opened negotiations with the enemy. Jane mounted the highest turret and turned her eyes towards the sea, with a last hope of seeing her deliverers. She descried some small specks far away in the distance. Rushing down into the street, she cried, with transports of joy :—

"Succours ! Succours ! The English succours ! No capitulation ! "

The English fleet soon entered the harbour, and a small but valiant body of English, headed by the chivalrous Sir Walter Manny, cast themselves into the town. The negotiations were at once broken off, and the besiegers, balked of their prey, renewed the attack with more determined vigour than ever.

Sir Walter and his companions were at dinner with the countess when a huge mass of stone crashed through the roof of an adjoining house, terrifying the ladies assembled in the castle hall. Starting from his seat, Sir Walter vowed to destroy the terrible engine which had thrown this missile. In a few moments the English sallied forth, hewed the monster catapult in pieces, burned the sow, and threw the enemy's camp into confusion. The foe, recovering from their first astonishment, tried to surround the returning warriors ; but the English knights stood their ground till the archers and men-at-arms had re-crossed the ditch. Then driving back their assailants they crossed the draw-bridge, and were received with acclamations by the towns-people, while the countess herself "came down from the castle to meet them, and with a most cheerful countenance kissed Sir Walter and all his companions, one after another, like a noble and valiant dame."

Prince Louis abandoned his camp the same evening, and retired to that of Prince Charles before the Castle of Arrai.

Charles, though unsuccessful in his attack on Hennebonne, soon became master of nearly the whole of Brittany. During the truce between England and France, the Countess de Montfort came to London, and asked King Edward to grant her further assistance. He commanded Robert of Artois to return with her, accompanied by a strong force, to Brittany. They encountered the French fleet near Guernsey; and during the engagement Jane displayed her accustomed bravery. The contending fleets were at last separated by a storm, and the English sailed to Brittany, took Vannes by storm, and massacred, not only the garrison, but even the townspeople. The French soon re-captured the town, when Robert of Artois was slain.

Edward III. landed in Brittany in 1345, with

twelve thousand men, but was not at first very successful. In June he was obliged to conclude a short truce with France, during which the Count de Montfort was set at liberty; but he died of a fever on Sept. 20th, when his son John was proclaimed duke. At the end of July, 1346, the English invaded Normandy. The Countess de Montfort, assisted by an English force under Sir Thomas Dagworth, defeated Charles of Blois, who was made prisoner.

Charles was set free in May, 1360, when peace was concluded between France and England. The treaty, though it did not interfere with Brittany, brought about an arrangement some months later, by which the duchy was divided between the rival claimants.

But Charles broke faith, and renewed hostilities with the assistance of France. The struggle was at last decided in favour of the Count de Montfort, by the death of Charles and his son John, both of whom were slain in the battle of Arrai, gained by the English, September 20th, 1364, the same day of the month on which his rival died.

The French heroine of this war was Julia du Guesclin, sister of the great Constable. When the English invaded Brittany to support the Count de Montfort, Julia, who was living with her sisters in a convent, was obliged to take refuge in the fortress of Pontsorel, which was soon besieged by the English.

The garrison was small and the besiegers were many, but Julia, with a courage worthy of her brother Bertrand, persuaded the French not to surrender. Clad in a coat of mail (one of her brother's) she stood on the ramparts and hurled back all who attempted to scale the walls. Animated by her courage, the French made so sturdy a defence that the English were compelled to retire, discomfited. Julia then commanded the garrison to throw open the gates and pursue the foe. The retreating army, confronted unexpectedly by a strong force commanded by the Constable himself, who was returning to Pontsorel, and surrounded on all sides, were nearly all slain, while their commander was made prisoner.

When the war was over, Julia returned to her convent, where she passed the rest of her days.

Another heorine of this war was Jane de Belleville. Her husband, Oliver, Lord of Clisson, was accused of holding secret intelligence with the English ; and in 1343 Philip de Valois, without waiting till the evidence should be well substantiated, caused him to be decapitated. The widow, burning for revenge, sold her jewels, and with the proceeds equipped three vessels. After sending her son, a lad of twelve, to England, to ensure his safety, Jane cruised about the coast of Normandy, attacking every French ship

which came in her way, and ravaging the country
for a mile or so inland. This female corsair was
frequently seen, with a sword in one hand and a
torch in the other, amidst the smoking ruins of a
castle, or the smouldering heaps of a destroyed
village, directing with inhuman exultation the
ferocious cruelties suggested by her thirst for
vengeance.

While King Edward and Philip de Valois were
devastating France in their contests for the crown,
the Romagna was the scene of a fierce struggle
between the Pope, the Visconti, and the various
nobles and cities of Italy. After having lost a great
part of his territories, Innocent II. reconquered the
States of the Church by means of the Cardinal
Legate Egidius Albornez. But the Papal governors
were so tyrannical that the nobles of the Romagna,
with few exceptions, fought desperately to maintain
their independence. Francesco d'Ordelaffi, lord of
Forli, was the last to give way. He was ably
seconded in his brave resistance by Marzia, his wife,
a member of the house of Ubaldini. While he was
defending Forli he entrusted the town of Cesena to
his wife; and in the beginning of 1357 the husband
and wife separated. Marzia took up her station in
Cesena, with a garrison of two hundred knights and
an equal number of common soldiers. She was

accompanied by her son and daughter, and by Sgariglino de Petragudula, the wise counsellor of the Ordelaffi family.

The town was soon invested by a force ten times as numerous as the garrison. At the end of April some terrified burgesses opened the gates of the lower town. But Marzia, recollecting the words of her husband, who declared that unless the Pope offered him honourable terms he would sustain a siege in every one of his castles, that when they were all taken he would defend Forli, the walls, the streets, his own palace, even to the last tower of his palace, before surrendering his rights, retreated to the upper town with those soldiers and towns-people who remained faithful. Sgariglino having proved to be a traitor, she caused him to be executed; his reeking head was flung from the battlements amongst the besiegers.

Marzia took upon herself all the duties of governor and military commander. She wore her helmet and cuirass day and night, and scarcely closed her eyes at all. At last she was compelled to retire into the citadel with four hundred soldiers and citizens who swore to stand by her to the death. But the citadel, undermined by the Papal engineers, almost hung in the air. Marzia's father, permitted by the legate, entered Cesena and besought her to surrender. Her answer was firm and simple. Her husband gave her a duty to perform, and she must obey implicitly.

At last the people began to murmur. Marzia was compelled to surrender. She conducted the negotiations herself; and so skilfully did she manage, that the Legate, afraid of driving her to despair, consented that her soldiers should return home unmolested, with their arms and accoutrements. On the 21st of June she opened the gate of the citadel.

She had disdained to make terms for herself, so the legate cast Marzia and her children into prison.

It is curious to note that there are now no remains of Cesena to commemorate the heroic valour of Marzia.

The illustrious northern heroine, Margaret, whose military achievements gained for her the title of " Semiramis of the North," was daughter of Waldemar, King of Denmark, and was born at Copenhagen in 1353. On the death of her father, Margaret, through her exceeding popularity with the people, succeeded in placing Olaus, her son, on the throne. Haquin, King of Norway, Margaret's husband, died in 1380, and Olaus in 1387. The election of a female sovereign was not yet authorised by custom; but Margaret's superior talents, her beauty, and her profuse liberality prevailed, and she was chosen

Queen of Denmark, and, soon after, she was elected Queen of Norway.

By taking advantage of the internal dissensions in the kingdom of Sweden, Margaret gained over a faction of the nobility, who offered her the crown. She marched into Sweden with a large army, and after a war of seven years defeated and captured King Albert at Falkœping. She kept him a prisoner seven years longer, at the expiration of which he resigned all claim to the Swedish crown.

To effect a permanent union of the three Scandinavian crowns, Queen Margaret concluded the famous Union of Calmar, 1397. She restored tranquillity at home, and was successful against all her enemies abroad; but her latter years were disturbed by the ingratitude of Eric, whom she had chosen as her successor. She died in 1412.

According to Border tradition, a Scottish maiden named Lilliard fought at the battle of Otterburn ("Chevy Chase") on the 19th of August, 1388, and displayed the same style of valour attributed to the gallant Witherington, who fell in the same battle. It is said that the following inscription was, till within a few years ago, to be seen on her tombstone :—

"Fair Maiden Lilliard lies under this stane,
Little was her stature, but great was her fame,
On the English lads she laid many thumps,
And when her legs were off, she fought upon her stumps."

One of the most faithful adherents of Henry
Bolingbroke in his days of adversity was Sir John
de Pelham, who had been squire to old John of
Gaunt. When Lancaster was banished by king
Richard, Pelham followed him abroad, leaving
Pevensey castle in charge of his wife, Lady Joan.
Sir John was one of the fifteen lances who disembarked at Ravenspur, in July, 1399, with Henry;
and on the 4th of the same month, while he was
sharing the fatigues and perils of what seemed then
a rash enterprise, the partizans of Richard II. laid
siege to Pevensey castle. Lady Joan, a noble and
spirited woman, took upon herself the conduct of the
defence, and directed all the efforts of the garrison
with such prudence and decision that the besiegers
were forced to retire.

When the Duke of Lancaster ascended the throne
as Henry IV., he remembered the services of his
faithful adherents. Sir John de Pelham was created
a Knight of the Bath, and appointed royal sword-
bearer, treasurer-at-war, and chief butler to the king.
The king further displayed his confidence in Sir
John by sending James I. of Scotland as a prisoner

9—2

to Pevensey castle. The courage of Lady Joan was
also publicly recognised and applauded.

Eric, Margaret's successor on the Scandinavian
throne, proved to be a very inferior ruler to his
illustrious aunt.  Nearly all his reign was taken up
with an inglorious war for the Duchy of Schleswig.
The quarrel was decided in favour of Denmark by
the Emperor Sigismund; but the Count of Holstein
refused to accept the imperial decree, and the war
waxed fiercer every day.  The Hanseatic League,
whose fleet then ruled the Baltic, joined the alliance
against Denmark; and in 1428 a powerful armament,
commanded by Count Gerard of Holstein, invested
Copenhagen.  The city would doubtless have fallen
but for the courage of Eric's queen, Philippa, who
was the daughter of Henry IV. of England.  Throwing herself into the city, the queen, by her exhor-
tations and example, inspired the garrison with such
enthusiasm and patriotic fervour, that the foe were
compelled to retire discomfited.

Elated by her success, Philippa now resolved to
carry the war into the enemy's country.  So, while
Eric was endeavouring to gather reinforcements of
men and money in Sweden, the queen, with a fleet
of seventy-five sail, invested Stralsund.  But this
time fortune was against the heroine.  The Danish
navy was almost entirely destroyed in a great sea-

fight. Eric, without reflecting that he had himself suffered many a worse defeat, flew into a rage when he heard of this disaster; and carried away by his blind fury, he even struck the queen. The high-spirited Philippa, unable to forgive this brutality, retired to a convent, where she died shortly after.

## VII.

Jeanne d'Arc, the Maid of Orleans —Margaret de Attendoli, Sister of the great Sforza — Bona Lombardi and Onerata Rodiana, Female Condottieri—Marulla (Turks in Europe)— Margaret of Anjou—Jeanne Hachette — Doña Aldonza de Castillo, and Doña Maria Sarmiento (Civil Wars in Castile)— Isabel the Catholic—Caterina Sforza.

T the beginning of the fifteenth century there dwelt in the little village of Domremy, on the banks of the Meuse, Jacques d'Arc, or Darc, a peasant, and Isabeau Romie, his wife. Though comparatively poor, they had the respect of their neighbours as being a hard-working, honest couple. They had three sons and two daughters, all of whom were bred, like their parents, to humble occupations. Joan, Jeanne, or Jehanne was born, according to different writers, in 1402, 1410, or 1412. She was

*Female Warriors.* **135**

exceedingly beautiful, with fine expressive features, and jet black hair. She was about the middle height, with a delicately moulded frame. Her education was the same as that of most peasant-girls, French or English, in those days—spinning, sewing, and repeating her Paternoster and Ave Maria. From her infancy Jeanne was employed in various duties, the chief of which was driving the cattle to and from pasture. She was of a religious, imaginative dispostion, and as early as her thirteenth year began to indulge those superstitious reveries which afterwards made her famous. Although her gentleness caused her to be universally beloved, she shunned girls of her own age, and took but little interest in the amusements of others. While her young friends were playing under the " Fairies' Tree " near the fountain of Domremy, Jeanne was dancing and singing by herself in pious fervour, or weaving garlands for the Holy Virgin in the small chapel of Notre Dame de Bellemont.

The villagers of Domremy were, without exception, staunch Royalists, while those of the neighbouring hamlet were zealous Burgundians. A very bitter hostility prevailed between the rival parties. On one occasion a band of troopers invaded Domremy and drove all the people from their homes. The family of Jeanne found shelter for a few days at an inn ; whence arose the mistake of the English chroniclers, who state that the maiden was in early life an innkeeper's servant.

For a quarter of a century, France had been torn by civil war, and the death of Charles VI. in 1422 plunged the country into hopeless confusion and anarchy. According to the Treaty of Troyes (concluded in 1420), Henry VI. of England was proclaimed King of France, which his uncle, the Duke of Bedford, governed as regent. Queen Isabella and the Duke of Burgundy joined England; and the Dauphin, abandoned by his own mother, had a very small party indeed. The English army was commanded by several brave and talented warriors—the Earls of Salisbury, Somerset, Warwick, Suffolk, Shrewsbury, Arundel, and many gallant knights.

The Dauphin, at the age of nineteen, was crowned at Poitiers, as Charles VII. On the 12th of October, 1428, the Earl of Salisbury laid siege to Orleans, the last stronghold of any importance held by the Royalists. It was bravely defended by Glaucour, Lahyre, and Dunois. Repeated messages were sent to the king imploring assistance. The city was naturally strong, and well-garrisoned, but the English commenced an elaborate system of counter-fortification, and cut off the supplies of the besieged.

Jeanne d'Arc watched with eager anxiety the siege of Orleans. Even as a child she had learned to detest the English; and now she felt herself commanded, by frequent visions and supernatural admonitions, to undertake the deliverance of her king and country. Believing firmly that Heaven destined her to save France, she refused more than one advantageous offer of marriage. In February, 1429, being then, according to the most reliable authorities, barely eighteen, she was commanded by a vision of Our Lady to raise the siege of Orleans, and afterwards conduct Charles to Rheims to be crowned in state. She presented herself before Robert de Baudricourt, governor of Vaucoulour, a town situated a few miles from Domremy, and related her mission. Believing her to be insane, the governor twice sent her away, threatening the second time to box her ears; but when she returned a third time he thought it best to send her with letters of recommendation to the Dauphin, at Chinon, in Touraine.

The fame of Jeanne d'Arc preceded her; and the king awaited with impatience the arrival of his extraordinary visitor. Although Charles disguised himself and mixed with his courtiers, Jeanne singled him out at once, and addressed him as king of France.

After being subjected to the most severe examination during three weeks, by divines, counsellors of parliament and learned men, the king was satisfied that her story was true, and consented to accept her aid. She was furnished with a suit of armour, and armed with a sword marked on the blade with five crosses, taken by her directions from the tomb of an old warrior in the church of St. Catherine at Fierbois. In company with several nobles she was sent to the camp at Blois, thirty-five miles from Orleans. Her presence produced the most miraculous effect upon the drooping spirits of the soldiers. The French generals resolved now to make some great effort for the relief of Orleans; and ten thousand men, commanded by St. Severre, Lahyre, and the veteran Dunois were despatched to its aid. Most of the soldiers retreated in dismay when they saw the strong towers of the besiegers, but La Pucelle, followed by a small party, forced her way through the English camp, and entered Orleans on the 29th of April, 1429. She was clad in armour and mounted on a snow-white horse; her head was bare, and the long raven tresses, parted across her forehead, were tied at the back with ribbon. In her right hand she grasped a lance; by her side hung the consecrated sword and a small battle-axe.

On the 4th of May a sortie was made against the English bastille of St. Loup, but the French were driven back with great slaughter. Jeanne, hearing the noise of the fight, mounted her horse and galloped to the spot, when she rode into the midst of the battle. The French, re-animated by her presence, again charged the English, drove them back, and captured the bastille.

After this first success the rest was comparatively easy. On the 6th and 7th the remaining bastilles on the south bank of the Loire were carried by storm. The most important, that at the head of the bridge, defended by Sir William Gladsdale with five thousand picked men, yielded after an attack of fourteen hours. During the attack on this tower, Jeanne, having placed a ladder against the walls, was attempting to scale the battlements, when she was struck in the neck by an arrow. She plucked out the weapon immediately, but the loss of blood compelled her to leave the field. However, when she heard that her absence dispirited the soldiers, she insisted upon returning to the scene of action.

The Earl of Salisbury died during the siege; and the Earl of Suffolk, who succeeded to the command, raised the siege on the 8th of May, and beat a hasty retreat.

Jeanne d'Arc, the "Heaven-sent Maid," had now fully entered upon her extraordinary career of victory. The universal belief in her elevated mission—as much amongst the English as the French—produced marvellous results. Resolute and chivalrous, pious and gentle, she won the hearts of all,—even the roughest and most sceptical veterans. However, it was only in matters of moral discipline that she was implicitly obeyed; oaths or foul language were severely censured when they

reached her ears. She compelled the entire army,
generals and soldiers alike, to attend regularly at
confession ; and at every halt she ordered an altar
to be established and the Holy Sacrament admini-
stered. But the generals, while they skilfully
employed her to animate the soldiers, did not
implicitly follow her counsels in military matters.

Her tactics were very simple. "I used," she
said, "to say to them 'go boldly in among the
English,' and then I used to go boldly in myself."
Her duties were chiefly confined to bearing at the
head of the army the consecrated sword and the
sacred banner—the latter made of white satin,
semée with fleurs-de-lis, with the words "Jesus
Maria," and a representation of Our Saviour in his
glory embroidered on its surface. Her conduct was
never stained by unfeminine cruelty. It appears
from the documents relative to her trial, that,
although she was herself wounded many a time,
she never shed the blood of anyone. Some French
historians, however, aver that she did sometimes,
when hard pressed, use the consecrated sword as a
weapon of offence.

When the Earl of Suffolk retired from before
Orleans he established his head-quarters at Méhun-
sur-Loire, and afterwards at Jargeau. Jeanne
hastened to Tours, where Charles was residing with
his court, and urged him at once to go to Rheims to

be crowned. The royal advisers, however, were afraid to venture on such a step when Rheims itself, together with all the intermediate towns, was still held by the English. The French next attacked the towns in possession of the English on the banks of the Loire. During the assault on Jargeau, which was taken by storm, La Pucelle, leading on the French, was seen on the highest step of one of the scaling-ladders, waving her banner over her head. A stone from the English engines struck her so violent a blow on the head, that her helmet was shattered, and she fell heavily to the foot of the wall. Rising on the instant, she cried :—

"Amis, amis! sus, sus! Notre Seigneur a con-damné les Anglais. Ils sont à nous. Bon courage!"

The Earl of Suffolk was made prisoner during the assault.

Beaugency and Méhun capitulated shortly after the fall of Jargeau; and the English, commanded by Talbot, Earl of Shrewsbury, the "English Achilles," retreated towards Paris. They were pursued and overtaken in April, 1429, at Patai, by the Maid of Orleans. Sir John Fastolfe, one of the bravest knights of his day (whatever Shakespeare may declare to the contrary), advised Talbot to continue his retreat with all speed; but the Earl scorned to fly before his enemies, even though, as on this occasion, they were twice as numerous as his own men. The

English, struck with a superstitious dread of La Pucelle, fled, after making little resistance; and Talbot, after losing twelve hundred men, was captured. Eight hundred English were slain in the pursuit. Sir John Fastolfe, with a prudence long stigmatised as rank cowardice, continued his retreat to Paris, where he arrived safely without the loss of a man.

Jeanne now insisted that the royal coronation should be no longer delayed. Every obstacle vanished at her approach. Troyes, Chalons, and other cities in rapid succession opened their gates; the people of Rheims expelled the English garrison, and Charles entered in triumph, July 16th, 1429. The consecration took place next day in the cathedral. The Maid stood by the side of Charles, clad in armour; and, taking the office of High Constable, held the sword over the king's head.

Her mission being now concluded, Jeanne d'Arc entreated the king's permission to "return to her father and mother, to keep her flocks and herds as before, and do all things as she was wont to do;" but her presence was considered so necessary to animate the troops, that she was prevailed upon to stay. In September, Jeanne was wounded in an unsuccessful attack on Paris, when she requested, a second time, to be allowed to retire from the war. But she was again overruled. In December, a patent of nobility was conferred upon her; she was first styled Dalis, then Dulis, and finally Dy Lys. Her coat of arms contained two golden lilies and a sword, pointing upwards, bearing a crown. She obtained for the villages of Domremy and Greux an exemption from taxation, which they enjoyed until the equalisation of public imposts in 1789.

In the spring of 1429, the Duke of Burgundy besieged Compiégne. Jeanne d'Arc threw herself into the town on the 21st of May. Believing that her presence now would work the same miracles as of old, she insisted, the evening of her arrival, that the garrison should make a sortie. After some hard fighting the French took to flight. Jeanne took the command of the rear-guard, and tried to rally her countrymen. A Burgundian archer pulled her from her horse; and while lying on the ground she was obliged to surrender to Lyonnel, the Bastard of Vendôme. There is good reason for supposing that Guillaume de Flavy, governor of the fortress, envious of her military renown, betrayed Jeanne into the hands of her enemies.

The English purchased Jeanne from the Duke of Burgundy for ten thousand livres; and Henry VI. also settled an annuity of three hundred francs upon her captor. Through many weary months the Maid of Orleans dragged out a miserable existence in a dungeon. In place of being treated as a prisoner of

war, she was handed over to ecclesiastical justice,
charged with heresy and blasphemy. At the insti-
gation of several Frenchmen a process was instituted
by the Bishop of Beauvais, in whose diocese she
had been captured. The process lasted three months
and had sixteen sittings. Jeanne denied resolutely
the accusations of sorcery and witchcraft, and named
St. Michael, St. Margaret, and St. Catherine as the
bearers of the heavenly messages.

The Bishop's Court, representing the Church and
the University of Paris, condemned Jeanne d'Arc
as a sorceress and a heretic. Charles VII. made
little or no efforts to save her; and after four
months' imprisonment, the innocent enthusiast was
sentenced to be burned alive at Rouen. She was
cut off from the Church, and delivered to the secular
judges.

On the 24th of May, 1431, she was carried to the
stake, which had been erected in the Vieux Marché of
Rouen. At sight of the pile her courage deserted her.
She submitted to the Church, and confessed that her
visions were the work of Satan. Her punishment
was commuted to imprisonment for life, but it was
not considered expedient to let her live; so she was
condemned as a relapsed heretic, and dragged to the
stake, May 30th. She was dressed in female attire;
and on her head was a mitre, covered with the words
"Apostate," "Relapse," "Idolâtre," "Hérétique."

She met her fate this time with terrible calmness. While they were putting the cap on her head, she said to one of the Dominican friars who stood by her side :—

" Maître, par la grâce de Dieu,·je serai ce soir en paradis."

Falling on her knees, she prayed fervently for a few moments, not for herself only, but for the ungrateful king who had so cruelly deserted her. The judges, even the stern Bishop of Beauvais, were moved to tears. She was burned by a slow fire, and the pile was so high that her agony lasted for a considerable time. Her ashes were gathered together and flung into the Seine.

There is a legend that, as she expired, a white dove rose from the flames. Another tradition says that after her ashes were removed, the heart was found entire.

The Rouen theatre now occupies that part of the public square on which the stake was erected. It was remarked as a curious coincidence that when Soumet's tragedy of " Jeanne d'Arc " was performed at Rouen, in the autumn of 1865, the last act, which represents the death of the Maid, was played on the identical spot where the real tragedy had been enacted in 1431.

Jeanne's father died of grief at her cruel fate ; her mother survived for many years, supported by a pension from the city of Orleans. In 1436 an impostor started up, who pretended to be the Maid of Orleans, giving a plausible account of her escape. She was for sometime successful, being acknowledged, even by the brothers, as the heroine herself. Within the last few years this idea of Jeanne's escape has been revived. Many French writers assert that there is ample documentary evidence to prove that the Maid of Orleans lived to be comfortably married, while another girl took her place at the stake. This notion is gaining ground, both in France and England.

Among all the divines who condemned Jeanne, there was only one Englishman—the Bishop of Winchester, Cardinal Beaufort.

In 1450 and 1451 measures were taken to revise the process of condemnation. In 1456 a court, presided over by the Archbishop of Rheims and the Bishops of Paris and Coutance, decided that Jeanne d'Arc was entirely innocent, and declared her to have been falsely condemned.

The citizens of Orleans celebrate the annual Festival of Jeanne d'Arc on the 8th of May; the villagers of Domremy hold an annual fête on the 6th of January, the birth-day of the heroine. It is said that the girls of the village have so much military *esprit* that they will hardly deign to look upon a lover who has not served some years in the wars.

The memory of Jeanne d'Arc has been preserved in France by several monuments. Louis XI. erected a figure of the heroine in front of her father's house; and in September, 1820, another memorial was raised in Domremy, with Jeanne's bust carved in marble. In the market-place of Rouen stands another figure of the Maid. In front of the Mairie of Orleans is a statue, modelled by the Princess Marie, daughter of the Citizen King. In April, 1855, a colossal equestrian figure was uncovered in one of the public squares of Orleans, on the exact spot where she animated the French soldiers to attack the foe. It was remarked as a sign of the times that not only the English flag, but also the Turkish crescent stood out prominently from amongst the numberless standards which surrounded the monument.

It has lately been proposed by the Bishop of Orleans, the Cardinal Archbishop of Rouen, and others, to add Jeanne d'Arc to the calendar of French saints. Shakespeare may thus prove once more a prophet; he has put into the mouth of King Charles, the words:—

> " No longer on Saint Denis will we cry,
> But Joan la Pucelle shall be France's saint."

During the fourteenth and fifteenth centuries Italy was terribly harassed by bands of mercenary soldiers,

who sought service in every war, and fought neither
through patriotism nor for the love of glory, but
merely for pay and the opportunity of plunder. These
bands, who counted their numbers by hundreds or
thousands, according to the reputation of the Condottiere (leader) under whom they fought, offered
their services to the prince or city that paid them
best, without regard to law or justice. Many of the
Condottieri, such as the Count of Werner, Montreal,
Bracchia de Montone, and Francesco Sforza, became
famous throughout Italy, not only as able generals,
but sometimes even as skilful statesmen ; yet, mostly
they were ignorant, brutal men, with nothing to
recommend them beyond reckless bravery.

Sforza had a sister named Margaret de Attendoli,
who shared his warlike spirit and enterprising courage. The family was of humble origin, but through
the military genius of Francesco it rose, by rapid
strides, to the highest rank and eminence. Before he
assumed the sovereignty of Milan, Sforza was grand-
constable of Naples; and in this capacity he was
sent to meet the Count de la Marche, the betrothed
husband of the Neapolitan queen. The count,
dreading the power of Sforza, caused him to be cast
into prison, with many of his relations. Sforza's
sister was at Tricario with her husband, Michael de
Cotignola, when the intelligence of Francesco's arrest
reached her. The relatives speedily assembled an

army, Margaret took the command, and a revolt
began. According as the Count de la Marche grew
more brutal towards his queen and more despotic to
her subjects, the insurrection became more general;
and at last Count Jaques was besieged in his castle.
The besiegers demanded that Sforza should be set at
liberty, and that the count should be content with
the title of lieutenant-general of the kingdom; but he,
knowing the value of his prisoner as a hostage, sent
threatening messages to Margaret, demanding that
Tricario should be given up, unless she would wish
to be the cause of her brother's death. Margaret,
indignant at the proposal, took the bold step of
imprisoning the deputies, whose families, alarmed for
their safety, importuned the count night and day,
till he consented to set Sforza at liberty, and rein-
state him in all his honours.

Female Condottieri were by no means uncommon
in those days; and some of the women acquired
celebrity, even beyond the Italian borders, for their
prowess and military skill. The story of one of these
female soldiers is interesting.

About the year 1432, Captain Brunoro, a Parmesan
gentleman by birth, and a Condottiere by profession,
was appointed by Piccinio, the Milanese general
(who had just driven the Venetians from Vatellina),
to maintain a camp in Morbego, as a central position

whence he could command the conquered territory.
While thus employed, he occupied his leisure time
with hunting, and various open air amusements.
One day, being tired, he stopped to rest in a sylvan
grove, where some peasants were celebrating a rustic
festival.   Doubtless there were many pretty faces
there; but one amongst them struck him more than
all the rest.   He entered into conversation with this
pretty girl, who charmed and surprised him by her
lively, spirited answers.

On his return home he learned that the pretty
peasant was quite a celebrity in the neighbourhood.
Her name was Bona Lombardi (or, as some give it,
Longobarba), and she was born in 1417, in the little
village of Sacco, in Vatellina.   She was the only
daughter of humble people, of whom little is known
except that her father, Gabriel Lombardi, was a
private soldier in one of the Italian armies, and died
while Bona was a child.   Her mother did not long
survive; and the little girl was left to the care of her
uncle, a poor priest, and her aunt, an industrious
countrywoman.

Captain Brunoro remained in Morbego during the
summer, and had thus frequent opportunities for
meeting with Bona Lombardi.   At last he decided
that she was the woman of all others to make him
happy, and they were married.   The marriage was
kept secret for some time; but to avoid even a

temporary separation, Bona dressed herself in the costume of a Condottiere, and accompanied her husband in all his expeditions.

Like all Condottieri Brunoro was obliged to adopt various masters ; and thus he very often found himself opposed to one of his former employers. Once he made an enemy of Alexander, King of Naples, who took him prisoner by means of an ambuscade, and cast him into prison. He would probably have ended his days in a Neapolitan dungeon, but for the untiring efforts of his wife. Money, entreaties, threats, all were employed ; till at last she procured his release.

Bona learned the art of war to perfection. Her courage and military skill were so highly esteemed by the Venetians that they confided to her and her husband the defence of Negropont, against the Turks, who in those days were dreaded by the Christians as much as the Goths and Vandals were in ancient times. More than once she displayed valour and prudence of a superior order. During the Milanese war, the Venetians having been repulsed in an attack upon the Castle of Provoze, in Brescia, Brunoro was captured. Bona arrived soon after with a small body of fresh troops. Rallying the discomfited Venetians, she led them in person to a second assault on the castle. This time they were successful, and Bona had the pleasure of releasing her husband with the rest of the prisoners.

Brunoro died in 1468, and Bona Lombardi, declaring that she could not survive her husband, built a tomb for the reception of their mutual remains. When it was finished, she sank into a state of languor, from which she never recovered.

Onerata Rodiana, another female Condottieri, was, in addition, a celebrated painter. She was born, in the early part of the fifteenth century, at Castelleone, and while yet a girl her reputation as a painter became so great that the Marquis Gabrinio, tyrant of Cremona, engaged her to decorate his palace.

One day, while thus occupied, a dissipated courtier, who happened to see her painting the walls of a room, attempted to take liberties. A struggle ensued, which was terminated by Onerata drawing a stiletto and stabbing her antagonist. She then fled from the palace, disguised herself in male attire, and quitted the city. Meeting with the band of Oldrado Sampuynano, the Condottiere, she enlisted under his banner.

The marquis was furious when he discovered the flight of his court-painter, and he despatched soldiers in pursuit. Soon relenting, however, he issued a proclamation, in which he promised full pardon on condition that Onerata would return to her professional labours. But she preferred the life of a soldier,

so she remained with her new comrades. By her
courage she soon rose to the post of captain ; and
for thirty years she led the roving life of a free-lance,
painting and fighting alternately. When Castelleone,
her native town, was besieged by the Venetians in
1472, she hastened with her band to its assistance.
She was victorious ; but during the action she fell,
mortally wounded.

In those days the Grecian isles were a constant
subject of contention between Venice and the Turks.
The latter, growing stronger every day, soon made
their name the terror of southern Europe. A few
years after the fall of Constantinople (captured by
Mohammed II. in 1453), the Ottomans besieged
Coccino, capital of the isle of Lemnos, in the Ægean
Sea. The city was defended with the most obstinate
bravery by the inhabitants, men and women.
Amongst the bravest of the women was Marulla, a
beautiful, noble-looking creature, barely in her
twentieth year. Her father, Demetrius, slew such
numbers of the Turks that the gateway was half-
blocked up with turbaned corpses. At last, pierced
with myriad wounds, he fell on the bodies of his
foes. Marulla, flying to her father's rescue, was
wounded by the same blow which proved fatal to
him ; but so far from giving way to useless lamenta-
tions, she seized his sword, sprang from the walls,

and fiercely attacked the Turks. Her fellow-citizens, inspired by her fire, drove the Turks away with terrific slaughter, and compelled them to take refuge in their ships.

When the Venetian admiral arrived next day with the fleet, in place of a beleagured town he beheld the citizens in their holiday attire, headed by the magistrates in their robes of state, marching in procession to meet him, conducting the heroine Marulla, their deliverer.

To reward her bravery, the Venetian commander ordered each of his soldiers to give her a present, and he promised that she should be adopted by the Republic. He offered her the hand of any one of his captains that she might prefer. But Marulla replied that "it was not by chance that she should choose a husband ; for the virtues of a camp would not make a good master of a family ; and the hazard would be too great."

When the Venetian senate received the news of Marulla's bravery, they decreed that various privileges and exemptions from taxes should be settled upon her and her children for evermore.

Henry VI., after losing the crown of France through a female warrior, very nearly saved the crown of England though another ; and, what is more remarkable, both were Frenchwomen. But the

high-spirited, fierce Margaret of Anjou, though fully
as brave, was very different from the peaceful, the
angelic Maid of Orleans. However, had the king
possessed half the spirit of his wife, the Wars of the
Roses might have terminated very differently. When
the feeble, almost imbecile king, wishing for peace
at any price, publicly acknowledged the Duke of
York as heir-apparent to the throne, Margaret refused her consent, and the war was renewed. Henry
was made prisoner in the battle of Northampton;
but the queen assembled a formidable army at York,
where she awaited her rival.

On the last day of the year 1460, the battle of
Wakefield was fought. Within half-an-hour of the
onset, nearly three thousand Yorkists lay dead on
the field. This battle, in which Margaret is said
to have taken an active part, terminated in a com-
plete victory for the House of Lancaster. The Duke
of York, covered with wounds, fell into the hands of
the victors. His dying moments were embittered by
the taunts of his captors; and afterwards, it is said,
his head was cut off by order of the queen, crowned
with a paper crown, and placed on one of the gates
of York.

The next year, 1461, Margaret defeated the Earl
of Warwick in the second battle of St. Alban's, and
recovered the king, who was now merely a passive
agent in the hands of friends or foes. She advanced

to London; but Edward, Earl of March, son of the Duke of York, having gained a victory at Hereford almost the same day as the battle of St. Alban's, obliged her to retreat towards the north. He then entered London, where a few days later, March 4th, 1461, he was proclaimed King of England, as Edward IV.

Margaret soon increased her army to sixty thousand men, and Edward was obliged to hasten to the north. At Pontefract he passed in review nearly forty-nine thousand men. The armies met at Towton, in Yorkshire, March 29th, 1461. This was the bloodiest battle fought during the war. No quarter was given or expected on either side. The Lancastrians, routed with fearful slaughter, were intercepted in their flight by the river; and the pursuit of the Yorkists was unrelenting. The slain amounted to thirty or forty thousand. Henry VI. and his brave queen fled to Scotland.

After vainly soliciting aid from the Scottish court, Margaret went over to France, and by promising to give up Calais, obtained ten thousand men. With these she landed in Scotland, where she was speedily joined by many of her partisans, and also by a band of freebooters. With these she entered England, and advanced to Hexham, where she was totally de-feated, May 15th, 1464, by Lord Neville.

The unhappy queen, compelled to fly with her

son, with difficulty reached the coast, after suffering indignities at the hands of the wild freebooters who infested the kingdom, and sailed for Flanders. The rebellion of Warwick the King-Maker, in 1470, restored Henry VI., for a few short months, to the throne. Edward IV. fled to the Continent; Margaret and her son landed at Weymouth on the very day (April 14th, 1471) that the Earl of Warwick was defeated at Barnet.

When Margaret heard the news of her champion's defeat her courage seemed at first to forsake her. She took refuge with her son in the sanctuary of Beaulieu, in Hampshire. But her undaunted spirit once more led her to the field. She re-assembled her partisans and marched to Tewkesbury, where she was encountered by King Edward on the 4th of May, 1471. The total defeat of the Lancastrians was the result, and Margaret, with her son, was made prisoner. The latter was cruelly murdered, and Margaret was placed in the Tower of London.

After remaining a prisoner for nearly four years, Queen Margaret was ransomed by Louis XI. for fifty thousand crowns. She died in 1482, "the most unfortunate Queen, wife, and mother," says Voltaire, "in Europe."

Charles the Bold, Duke of Burgundy, one of the greatest warriors of the Middle Ages, was brother-in-law to Edward IV., whom he assisted, in 1471, with men and arms; the English King promising, in return, to aid Charles against his great enemy, Louis XI. The French King was terribly afraid of the Duke; and had not the latter been so rash and the former so crafty, King Louis might have lost his crown. In 1472 Charles crossed the Somme at the head of eighty thousand men, and after capturing Nesle, where he massacred the people and burned the town, he laid siege, in June, to the town of Beauvais, in Picardy. The inhabitants were devoted to Louis XI., and, besides, they knew from the fate of Nesle, where the blood flowed "ankle-deep" in the street, what they might expect in the event of capture. So the defence was as stout as the attack was fierce.

There dwelt in Beauvais a girl named Jeanne Fourquet, born November 14th, 1454, the daughter of an officer in the king's guards. She was adopted, after her father's death, by a lady named Laisné. From childhood Jeanne had taken a great interest in tales of warlike valour; she always revered Jeanne d'Arc as a saint. She now displayed her military tendencies in such a way as to save her native town and immortalise her name. Arming herself with a *hachette*, or small axe, she placed herself at the head of a band of women, and led them to the ramparts, where they occupied themselves loading the cannon, pouring hot water, boiling oil, or molten lead on the heads of the besiegers, supplying the archers with arrows, or performing any other service their strength would allow.

The Burgundians at last planted their ladders, and commenced scaling the ramparts; but the first man who planted the flag of Charles was hurled from the battlements by Jeanne Fourquet, who snatched the standard from his hands, and waved it over her head. This deed so animated the defenders of Beauvais, that they gallantly repulsed every assault. After a fierce contest of nine hours, the besieged were reinforced by the garrison of Noyen, and on the two following days by troops and provisions from Amiens, Genlis, and Paris.

Charles battered the walls with heavy guns for nearly a month, and almost destroyed the town with fire-balls. Finding his troops still held at bay, he ordered a general assault on the 10th July, at seven in the morning. The attack was fierce, but the defence was resolute. The women, still led by Jeanne, displayed the same courage as before. Thrice the Burgundians scaled the walls, and planted their flag on the battlements; thrice they were repulsed with terrible losses. After the assault had lasted four hours, the Burgundians saw their efforts were fruitless, and sounded a retreat. During the night of the 22nd they broke up their camp, and marched away towards Normandy.

Jeanne Fourquet deposited the flag she had taken in one of the churches of Beauvais—doubtless that of the Jacobins, where it was preserved for many years. It may now be seen at the Hôtel de Ville. Louis XI. granted to her the privilege of bearing this standard at the head of the French army. Some years after this great event, Jeanne married Collin Pillon, when, not only was she herself exempted from taxation, but the same immunity was granted to her descendants.

It is neither by the name of Fourquet nor Pillon that the heroine is famous. The weapon with which she was armed gave her a more illustrious surname; and since that valiant deed, for which her countrymen must ever remember her with gratitude, she has been known as Jeanne Hachette.

Her portrait may still be seen at Beauvais; and in commemoration of her bravery, the anniversary of July 10th is celebrated by an annual procession, in which the women march before the men.

Napoleon III., when President of the French Republic, inaugurated a statue of Jeanne Hachette at Beauvais.

During the civil wars which agitated Castile towards the close of the century, the fortress of Toro was, by a curious coincidence, twice defended by female commanders, the wives of two brothers opposed to one another in politics. In 1475 it was held for Isabel the Catholic by Doña Aldonza de Castillo, wife of the Alcayde, Don Rodrigo de Ulloa, governor of the fortress. After the retreat of Ferdinand, husband of Isabel, she was compelled to surrender. In the following year the fortress was defended against the troops of Ferdinand and Isabel by Doña Maria Sarmiento, wife of Don Juan de Ulloa. All hopes of assistance having been dispelled, she obtained honourable terms of capitulation.

The same year, 1476, Isabel the Catholic having received intelligence that the Portuguese meditated invading her dominions, resolved to superintend in person the defence of the frontiers. Despite the remonstrances of her council, she set out for Estramadura in the summer of 1477, and, after capturing several fortresses, and placing strong garrisons in Badajoz, Ciudad Rodrigo, and other frontier towns, established her head-quarters at Seville.

Queen Isabel again displayed her wish to be a warrior during the contest between Ferdinand and the Moors. In 1487 and 1489 she encouraged the Spanish soldiers by her presence in the camp. In 1491 Ferdinand commenced the siege of Granada. Isabel arrived towards the close of May. Attired in a magnificent suit of armour, and mounted on a richly caparisoned horse, she rode through the ranks, greeted on all sides with joyful acclamations.

Wishing to obtain a nearer view of the renowned **red** towers of the Alhambra, the queen rode forward on the 18th June, escorted by the entire Spanish cavalry, to the village of La Zubia, situated at a short distance from Granada. But her curiosity was very near being the cause of her capture. A large body of Moorish troops sallied out from Granada and attacked the body-guard of the queen. Matters were growing serious, when the Marquis de Cadix came to the rescue with twelve hundred lances, and put the Moors to flight.

During the conflict Isabel did not display exactly the courage of a heroine. Struck with abject terror, she remained on her knees all the time, praying earnestly; and made a vow that if she escaped she would erect a monastery on the spot.

Most of the great Sforza's immediate descendants were more or less distinguished for military talents. Caterina, or Catherine, the natural daughter of Galeas Sforza, was remarkable for valour, military skill, and also for her personal beauty. She was the wife of Jerome Ricario, Prince of Forli; and some time after their marriage he was assassinated by Francis Del Orsa, who had revolted against him. Caterina and her children fell into the hands of the assassin, but she soon escaped to Rimini, which still remained faithful. She defended the town, in 1466, with such determination that the besiegers, to frighten her into a surrender, threatened to put her children to death.

Caterina was at last restored to sovereign power, and married John de' Medici, a man of noble family, though not very distinguished for genius or bravery. In 1500 she defended Forli against the talented Cæsar Borgia; being compelled to surrender, she was imprisoned in the castle of San Angelo, at Rome. Soon, however, she was restored to liberty; but her dominions were never given back to her. She died shortly after her release.

## VIII.

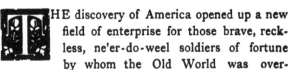

HE discovery of America opened up a new
field of enterprise for those brave, reckless, ne'er-do-weel soldiers of fortune
by whom the Old World was over-
run. Adventurers sailed from various ports of
Europe, under the command of audacious leaders,

such as Balboa and Pizarro, whose daring spirit and enterprising disposition gave them authority over their companions. Numbers of women, imbibing the spirit of the times, accompanied those bands of adventurers—sometimes disguised in male attire, but more frequently in the garments of their own sex.

When Cortez sailed from Cuba, in 1518, on that voyage which terminated in the conquest of Mexico, he was followed by six hundred soldiers, many of whom were accompanied by their wives. These Castilian dames, preferring to endure the hardships of a campaign than be separated from their husbands, and probably feeling curious to see for themselves those marvels of the New World about which all Europe was talking, in no way disgraced the name of Spaniard by any feminine timidity. In the camp before Mexico, which Cortez was besieging, 1521, it was their fortitude which kept up the spirit of the soldiers, who, repulsed in several assaults on the city, and suffering from famine, had become gloomy and despondent. Several examples have been preserved of the bravery displayed by these Spanish wives. One of them would frequently mount guard to relieve her tired husband; another, seeing the Spaniards repulsed in an attack, hastily donned a soldier's *escaupil*, snatched up a sword and lance, rallied the retreating Christians and led them once more against the Mexicans.

Cortez had requested the women to remain behind, at Tlascala, but they proudly answered him that " It was the duty of Castilian wives not to abandon their husbands in danger, but to share it with them—and die with them if necessary."

The name of one of these female warriors was Maria d'Estrada, who fought by the side of her husband through every campaign, displaying the same courage as her companions in arms.

Another Spanish-American heroine was Catalina de Erauso, the " Monja Alferez," or Nun-Lieutenant. Her life was the most romantic that could be imagined. She has written her own history in pure and classic Spanish, displaying as much literary ability in its composition as, in her warlike career, she had shown heroic valor, mixed with savage cruelty.

She was born in 1592, daughter of a Spanish hidalgo of St. Sebastian, Don Miguel de Erauso, an officer in the royal army, and, after the fashion of those days, was destined for the Church. So, at the early age of four, she was sent to the Dominican convent, the prioress of which was her aunt. Here she remained till her fifteenth year ; but during all these years she acquired so inveterate a dislike for the cloister that she contrived to make her escape from the convent, shortly before the day on which she was to take the veil. She hid in a chestnut grove for three days, cut her hair short, made her petticoats into male attire, and then started on her travels.

She passed through various romantic adventures in Spain, acting in the different capacities of page, clerk, and servant. Thus disguised, she joined an expedition to South America, where she became a soldier. At different times she assumed one name or another; but that under which she was best known, and was promoted to the rank of lieutenant, was Alonzo Dias. Under this alias she was the victor in several skirmishes. So clear was her judgment that her opinion was frequently asked by the generals at their councils of war.

During the intervals of military duty, Catalina gambled, drank, robbed, assassinated, cursed and swore, and behaved altogether very like an Alsatian bully. She chose for her associates the most desperate and reprobate characters, and seemed to take a fiendish delight in outdoing them. Sometimes she would pay attentions to a simple girl, and when the wedding-day was fixed she would disappear.

One night, in a gambling-house in Chili, she quarrelled with, and stabbed a gentleman of great importance in the city. The relatives made the place so hot for Catalina, that she was compelled to make her escape across the Andes, into another province. Her lawlessness once brought her under the

hands of the hangman ; and a reprieve arrived just
as, with the noose round her neck, she was about to be
launched into eternity. She wandered over every
part of Spanish America, taking up, at random, the
profession of soldier, sailor, or even lawyer.

The discovery of her sex was brought about by
a curious accident. Her violent deeds having again
provoked the guardians of the law, she was compelled to fly for refuge for sanctuary to a church at
Guámango, in Peru. The bishop, a pious man,
tried to convert the young criminal, animadverting
on the wicked life the latter had been leading, and
exhorting her to repentance. The stubborn heart
of Catalina, inured to every kind of reproach and
harsh language, was touched by the kindness with
which the bishop spoke. For a few moments she
maintained a dogged silence ; then, falling on her
knees and bursting into tears :—

"Father," she sobbed. "I am a woman!"

She then told the astounded prelate her extraordinary story. He pitied the unhappy young
woman, and by his influence she was pardoned and
permitted to return to Spain. She arrived at Cadiz
in 1624, whither her fame had preceded her.
During her journey through Spain and Italy the
streets were crowded by wondering spectators.
Pope Urban VIII. allowed her to retain her
masculine costume for the rest of her days. It is

not known in what year she died; according to an old
manuscript preserved in a convent at Vera Cruz,
she devoted her latter years to trade, and assumed
the name of Antonio de Erauso. Her portrait was
taken at Seville by Pacheco, a Spanish painter.

During the early years of the Emperor Charles
V.'s reign, the nobles of Castile formed a confederacy
called the Holy Junta, and took up arms to recover
their traditional rights and privileges. John de
Padilla, a young noble, was at the head of this
insurrection; but it was his wife, Doña Maria
Pacheco, who really conducted the confederacy.
She was highly gifted and extremely ambitious,
though, like most ambitious people, not at all
scrupulous as to the means employed, so long as the
event turned out according to her wishes.

The Junta soon began to languish for want of
money, so Doña Maria persuaded the people to strip
the cathedral at Toledo of its plate and jewellery.
In 1521 Padilla was captured, and sentenced to
death. He wrote to his wife, telling her not to
grieve, but rather to consider his death as his
deliverance from a weary life. But his capture
proved fatal to the confederacy. Toledo, the head-
quarters of the rebels, was soon invested by the
king's troops. Doña Maria used every means to
secure her position. She even wrote to the French

general on the Spanish frontier, inviting him to invade Navarre. By keeping the death of Padilla fresh in the minds of the citizens, she incited them to make a resolute defence. Sorties attended with varied success were made, sometimes daily, from the garrison.

At last the canons of the cathedral, whom she had offended, worked on the minds of the ignorant, credulous multitude, telling them that Maria's influence over them was due entirely to witchcraft. The loss of three hundred men in a desperate sortie so humbled the citizens that they drove Maria into the Alcazar, and opened the gates to Charles's troops.

Maria defended herself four months longer in the citadel. But at last, reduced to the utmost extremities, she fled into Portugal, where many of her relatives and friends resided, and there passed the remainder of her days in great poverty.

Eleonora of Toledo, the first Grand-Duchess of Tuscany, was a woman possessing great courage and a powerful, ambitious intellect. In 1543 she married Cosmo de'Medici, Duke of Florence. Eleonora took an active part in the wars between her husband and his hereditary enemies, the Strozzi; and in the bloody and terrible battles fought during the struggle, she never left him. Her courage aided greatly to turn the fortune of war. One day, while riding out with an escort of fifteen horsemen, she encountered Philip Strozzi, commander of her husband's enemies, reconnoitring the Florentine camp. Although he had a guard of forty-five men, Eleonora, with her accustomed bravery, attacked him, slew nearly all his men, and took himself prisoner. Philip, knowing that he could not expect quarter—which had never been granted to prisoners on either side during the war—committed suicide sooner than perish ignominiously on the scaffold. Eleonora was so shocked that she prevailed on her husband to spare the lives of his prisoners henceforth.

Eleonora also took a leading part in the war between Charles V. and Francis I. Together with her husband she was activly engaged in the storming of Sienna. She urged Cosmo to have himself crowned king; but he was unable to carry out her project. Pope Pius V. at length changed his title from Duke of Florence to Grand-Duke of Tuscany.

Eleonora's ambition being now satisfied, she gave up the rest of her life to the encouragement of the fine arts, national education, and founding charitable institutions. The date of her death is unknown.

Under Solyman the Magnificent, the Turks conquered the greater part of Hungary; whose king, Louis II., was routed and slain in the disastrous battle of Mohacz, 1526.   And during the next hundred and fifty years Hungary was the scene of endless strife between the Crescent and the Cross. For a long time victory inclined to the side of the infidels.   Women, as usual, took a prominent share in the terrible scenes of bloodshed and carnage. Wherever there was a town to be defended, women immediately took up arms and aided the men to keep off the common enemy.

This female courage showed itself on both sides during these dreary wars.   In 1529, during the absence of Solyman, the Christians laid siege to Buda, the capital of Hungary.   One day, having overpowered the Turks, they were rushing into the town, when a Jewess tearing a strip of rag from her gown, lighted it, and fired off an immense cannon which the Ottomans in their flight had overlooked. It caused such havoc amongst the Hungarians that they were paralyzed with terror—thus gaining time for the Janizaries to rally; and the result was the final repulse of the Christians.

Tradition declares that Solyman, when he heard of this courageous act, ordered the Jewess's gown to be girt with a circle of pure silver.

In 1552 Solyman besieged Temesvar, which was defended by the brave Lasonczy.   The wife of the latter led an army to the relief of her husband, and attacked the Turkish camp, but she was soon defeated. The revolt of the German garrison soon after compelled Lasonczy to surrender.

The town of Erlau, besieged at the same time, withstood gallantly the repeated assaults of a numerous army. Its fortifications were of the poorest description, and the garrison small, but the valour, the patriotism of the townspeople supplied every deficiency. Old men and young girls, sword and spear in hand, aided in the defence. One woman was fighting beside her husband when he fell, pierced by a Turkish bullet. Her mother, who was also assisting to defend the wall, now wished to remove the body, and suggested that they should devote themselves to seeing it honourably interred. But the young widow refused to leave the scene of action.

" May God," she cried, " never suffer the earth to cover my husband's corse, till his death has been amply avenged. This is the hour of battle, not a time for funeral and for tears."

She seized the shield and sword of her dead husband, and rushing upon the Turks, refused to leave the breach, till by the slaughter of . three infidels she had satisfied her thirst for revenge. Then she raised the corpse of her lord, and bore it to the principal church in the town, where she paid to it the last honours with great splendour.

When the Turks were besieging Alba, several

women, whose husbands had been slain, volunteered
to defend the walls. The Turks were amazed at
the cool bravery with which these female warriors
defended the various posts assigned to them. For
several hours they held a bastion, the possession of
which was deemed highly important by both Turks
and Christians. Every Turk who endeavoured to
scale the bastion had his head struck with a scythe.

For more than three months, thanks to the valour
of the women, the town of Valpon set the Mussul-
man power at defiance, backed though the latter
was by all the appliances of war.

The same resistance met them at Agria, not far
from Valpon, where the wives and daughters of the
citizens carried oil, pitch, boiling water, molten lead,
etc., to pour on the heads of the Turks. One
woman was struck down by a cannon ball just as she
was about to hurl a big stone on the skulls of the
infidels. Her daughter, seeing her fall, was filled
with the thirst for revenge. Rushing to the breach,
she fought with the desperate bravery of a lioness
deprived of her cubs, slaying and wounding on all
sides. At last she was herself slain. One of the
citizens fighting on the ramparts observed his son-
in-law struck dead by a musket-ball. Turning to
his wife, he asked her to carry away the corpse and
render to it the last offices.

"There is another duty more pressing," replied

she. "That of defending our religion and our country comes before love. To them I will give the last drop of my blood."

During the siege of Szigeth, in 1566, which cost the Turks twenty thousand men, orders were given one day for a general assault. A Hungarian officer, wishing to save his wife from falling into the hands of the infidels, took the cruel resolution of putting her to death. But his young wife, less attached to her life than to her husband, declared that she would accompany him to battle, there to receive death or glory. Dressing herself in a suit of his clothes, she armed herself and went with him to the field. No one displayed greater courage than she did. Without once quitting her husband, she slew every Turk who came within reach of her sword. She continued to fight with the same ardour till the close of the engagement, and wherever she was seen a Turkish corpse remained to mark her presence. At last her husband was slain, and she herself, severely wounded by the Turkish arrows, lay on her husband's breast. After receiving the last sacrament, she expired in great agony.

During the siege of Famagosta, in Cyprus, by Mustapha Pacha, in 1571, the noblest Cypriote dames, undismayed by the iron fire of the Turkish batteries, aided to defend the city. Not only did they carry round food and ammunition to the soldiers, but, during the assault, they rolled huge stones on the heads of the Turks assembled in the ditch below or climbing to the attack.

In the annals of French poetry few names stand higher than that of Louise Labé, *La Belle Cordière*. She was born at Lyons in 1526 or 1527. Nature was lavish in her gifts; to personal beauty and an exquisite voice, were added talents for literature and music. Her education included music, languages, riding, and military exercises. The last named acquirement excited in the mind of Louise a wish to enter the army. At the age of sixteen she served, under the name of Captain Loys, in the campaign of 1542, which ended in the siege of Perpignan. Some say she followed her father, others her lover to the field; but whatever was the cause of her presence in camp, she earned great praises for her courage. But the French were obliged to raise the siege; and Louise Labé, after sharing in the fêtes and tournaments held by the Dauphin, gave up the military profession, henceforth devoting her time to music and poetry.

She married Ennemond Perrin, a wealthy rope-maker, and thus acquired the opportunity to follow her literary inclinations. She possessed a valuable library of books in Greek, Latin, Spanish, and

Italian, which languages she knew perfectly. Her spacious and tastefully laid-out gardens became the resort of nobles, poets, savants, wits, artists, musicians, and men of genius of every kind; and at these re-unions the musical skill of *La Belle Cordière* showed to advantage. She excited at the same time the admiration of the poets and the envy of the ladies. The street in Lyons where she lived was christened after her. She died in 1566, one year after her husband, who had left her sole heir to his large property.

Her chief works were an " Epistle to Clemence de Bourges," the " Débat de la Folie et de l'Amour," a drama in prose, three elegies, and twenty-four sonnets. The first edition of her writings appeared in 1555.

Mary of Hungary, wife of the unfortunate Louis II., who was slain in the battle of Mohacz, was celebrated throughout continental Europe for her military prowess and her love of field-sports. From the latter she acquired the soubriquet of Diana, while from her habit of mixing with the soldiers she was styled (like the Empress Victoria) " Mother of the Camp." She was the daughter of Philip I. of Spain, and handsome even for a Spanish princess, majestic in her carriage, yet affable and charming in her manners. Her brother, the Emperor Charles V., had so high an opinion of her political abilities that he entrusted to her charge the government of the Netherlands; and her court soon became famous for the magnificence of its tournaments and spectacles.

Mary commanded during several expeditions against the troops of France; and during the various battles and skirmishes which ensued, she would frequently march on foot, or ride with the soldiers to encourage them by her presence. In 1553, when Charles V. was besieging Metz, which was defended by the Duke of Guise, Mary caused a diversion, by invading Picardy, to prevent Henry II. from succouring the besieged. By this raid she caused terrible havoc, destroying seven or eight hundred villages, and burning Folembrai, a favourite palace of Francis I.

Henry II., in retaliation, burned some of the most populous towns in the Netherlands, together with the royal palace of Bains, which was one of the architectural wonders of the age. Mary vowed that France should repent this deed. She kept her word; and more than once her conduct savoured of gross cruelty. Henry directed his soldiers to try their utmost to make Mary a prisoner; for, said he, he would like to try whether she would retain, in captivity, her haughty, courageous spirit.

Mary resigned the government of the Netherlands in 1555, and returned to Spain, where she died three years afterwards.

Graine-ni-Mhaile, Granu Weal, or Grace O'Malley, a famous Irish heroine who lived during the latter half of the sixteenth century, was daughter of Owen O'Malley, a noted chief who commanded a small navy. He used to make voyages from port to port, partly for commerce, but more especially for piracy. During childhood, Grace frequently accompanied her father on his expeditions. After his death, her brother being a minor, she took command of the galleys, and made several voyages. Her chief rendezvous was at Clare island, off the coast of Mayo, where she kept her larger vessels moored. Here, too, she had a fortress. Her smaller ships she kept at Carrigahooly Castle, which was her favourite residence, and chief stronghold.

Her piracies at length became so frequent and so daring that a reward of five hundred pounds was offered by the English Government for her apprehension. Troops were sent from Galway to Carrigahooly ; but after a siege of more than a fortnight, they were compelled to retire. The people of Connaught relate numerous adventures and extraordinary actions performed on the high seas by Granu Weal.

Her first husband was O'Flaherty, chief of West Connaught. After his death she married Sir Richard Burke, and became reconciled to the English. After her second marriage, she frequently assisted the

12—2

English with her troops in Connaught; for which Queen Elizabeth wrote her an autograph letter, thanking her and inviting her on a visit to the court, at London. Graine-ni-Mhaile, with several galleys, sailed to London in 1575. She was received with great distinction by the queen, who offered to make her visitor a countess; but Grace declined this honour, and answered with much spirit, that both of them being princesses, they were equal in rank, and could not therefore confer titles or honours upon each other. But, she said, her majesty might confer any rank she pleased on young Burke (son of Grace), who was born on board ship during the voyage to England; named from this circumstance, Tioboid-na-Lung, signifying Theobald of the Ships. Queen Elizabeth, it is said, knighted him under the title of Sir Theobald Burke; he was afterwards created Viscount of Mayo by Charles I.

On her voyage home Granu Weal landed at Howth for provisions. She was greatly surprised to find the gates of the castle closed, because the family were at dinner. Indignant at this dereliction from Irish hospitality, Granu seized a little boy whom she found playing with an attendant near the sea-shore. Finding that he was the infant heir of Howth, she brought him to Connaught: refusing to restore him till Lord Howth had entered into an agreement that his gates should never again be closed during dinner.

The abduction of the infant heir of St. Lawrence forms the subject of a painting at Howth Castle.

Grace O'Malley was buried in a monastery which she had herself endowed, on Clare island. There are yet some remains of her monument to be seen there. Her name has always been familiar in the mouths of Irish peasants; and she is still sung as a heroine in various ballads, English and Irish.

During the fiercely contested wars brought about by the efforts of the Roman Catholic princes to stop the Reformation, women, as usual, took their share of the dangers and privations endured by all for the sake of their faith. They displayed as much courage and fortitude as the men, whether, as the wives and daughters of citizens they aided to defend their homes, or whether as princesses they boldly headed their troops in defence of their religion and their dominions.

Kenan Simonsz Hasselaar was heroine of the famous siege of Haarlem. The revolting cruelty of Spain in her first efforts to stamp out the rebellion in the Netherlands, only stimulated the Dutch to bolder and more desperate efforts for freedom. Haarlem was one of the most important cities; and the Spaniards, resolved to capture it at any price, despatched twelve thousand men, commanded by Frederic of Toledo, to besiege the city in December,

1572. On the 12th, during a severe frost, the place was invested. Bravely did the inhabitants, both soldiers and citizens, resist the Spaniards. Women cheerfully shared in all the toils and dangers, the manifold privations of the defence.

Kenan Simonsz Hasselaar, a widow about fifty years old, of a noble family, raised a troop of three hundred women for the defence of the walls. At the head of her corps she was constantly seen pressing forward to attack the Spaniards, or aiding in the erection of new defences. Even the besiegers, who were repulsed with great slaughter in several assaults, could not help admiring the courage of this Amazon band.

Holland still holds the name of Kenan Hasselaar very dear. One of the ships launched from the government dock-yards every year receives her name. A huge painting suspended in the hall of the Haarlem Stadthuis transmits her glorious deeds to posterity; and her portrait hangs in the Treasure Chamber of the Municipality, amongst the commanders of St. John, the relics of the Spanish wars, the town insignia, and the other precious nick-nacks and antiquities collected together, accumulated by generations of thrifty and patriotic burghers.

The women of Alkmaar (which was besieged by Don Frederic immediately after the fall of Haarlem) displayed the same courage. During the general

assault made by the Spaniards on the 18th Septem-.
ber, 1573, the women aided the soldiers by hurling
down fragments of stones and red-hot iron, and pouring boiling oil, molten pitch, rosin, and lead on the
besiegers, of whom a terrible carnage was made.

Mary Queen of Scots, the unfortunate rival of
Elizabeth, was a high-spirited, courageous woman,
possessing great talents for ruling; and had she
lived before the Reformation, she might possibly
have been more successful than her ancestors, most of
whom came to an untimely end. But the bitter hostility of John Knox was too powerful for the queen,
though for some years she contrived to keep her throne.
In 1565, shortly before her ill-starred marriage with
Darnley, the Congregational citizens of Edinburgh,
stirred up to rebellion by the secret machinations of
the queen's " base brother, Moray," turned out in
hostile array, and encamped at St. Leonard's Crags.
Mary, undismayed by the fierce looks and big words
of these staunch Protestants, rode to meet them at
the head of a mere handful of troops. The rebel
leaders fled, and the rest, under promise of pardon,
returned to their homes.

In July of the same year the queen wedded
Darnley. This was the signal for an open insurrec-
tion on the part of the Scottish nobles. Again Queen
Mary showed herself a worthy descendant of the

Stuarts. " She acted in this emergency," remarks Miss Strickland, " with energy and spirit indicative of the confidence inspired by her popularity, and showed herself no whit behind the most distinguished of her predecessors in courage and ability." At the head of five thousand men she left Edinburgh, August 26th, together with her husband, the lords of the council, and her ladies-in-waiting. She was attired in a scarlet and gold-embroidered riding-habit, which, it was said, covered a light suit of armour, while her hood and veil were understood to conceal a steel casque. Pistols hung at her saddle-bow. Darnley, with a vanity inherent in his nature, wore a gorgeous suit of gilded armour.

On the 29th the queen reached Glasgow ; and next day the rebels retreated from Paisley towards Hamilton. The queen set out in pursuit. The confederate lords, disappointed in their expectations of a general Protestant rising, were obliged to retreat from place to place before the queen and her army. The bravery and endurance of Mary gained the love and respect of many amongst her subjects.

Mary returned to Edinburgh for a short time ; and on the 8th of October she marched again, this time at the head of eighteen thousand men, to renew the war. The rebel lords, terrified at the approach of their royal mistress, fled across the English border, and took refuge in Carlisle.

Queen Mary had no further opportunity of displaying her courage till after the murder of Darnley, in 1567, when the base conduct of Bothwell and the consequent insurrection of nearly all the Scottish nobles forced her once more to take the field in person. When the opposing armies met, June 14th, at Carberry Hill, she rode with her followers to the field, though neither she nor they had broken their fast that morning.

After this followed the captivity of Mary in Loch-Leven Castle. In 1568 she made her escape, and assisted by a few friends, made a last effort to recover her throne. The Earl of Murray (regent during the minority of king James), with a large army intercepted the queen's march at Langside, two miles from Glasgow.

It is not quite clear whether Mary took an active part in the battle of Langside, which for ever crushed her hopes. Brantôme declares "the Queen-mother of France assured him that Mary mounted her good hackney and rode into the battle like another *Zeno-bia*, to encourage her troops to advance, and would fain have led them to the charge in person. But she found them all quarrelling among themselves, and insensible to her eloquence, and more inclined to exchange blows with each other than to attack the rebel host."

According to the popular tradition, however, it

was beneath the spreading boughs of a hawthorn, which is still known as " the Queen's thorn," half-way up the green hill behind Castlemilk, that the unfortunate sovereign stood and watched the battle, surrrounded by her ladies and a few devoted adherents. Legend also points out another " Queen's thorn " on the hill behind the ruins of Cathcart Castle. According to a local history, Lord Living-stone, at the head of "the bairns of Falkirk," rode with the queen to the battle-field, and afterwards aided her to escape; and this would seem to corroborate what Brantôme has said.

Amongst those heroines who distinguished them-selves during the religious wars in France, was Magdalaine de Saint-Nectaire,—also called Se' nectaire, or Sennetaire. She was a staunch Protest-ant, and after the death of her husband, Gui di Saint Exuperi, she retired to her château at Miremont, in Limousin, armed sixty of her retainers, and commenced a series of raids against the Roman Catholics. In 1575, during the reign of the weak and frivolous Henry III., Montal, Lieutenant du Roi, in Limousin, whose soldiers had often been defeated by Magdalaine, resolved to besiege the heroine in her château. With fifteen hundred foot and two hundred horse he arrived before the gates. Mag-dalaine made a sally, and cut to pieces a detach-

ment of fifty men; but on her return she found that
the château had been captured. She gallopped to
Turene, a neighbouring town, to gather reinforcements, returning thence with four companies of
mounted arquebusiers. Montal awaited her in a
defile of the mountains; but he was vanquished and
mortally wounded. His soldiers, discouraged by the
fall of their leader, withdrew the same evening to a
neighbouring castle, where Montal died four day's
later.

The year of this heroine's death is not recorded.

Another heroine of these wars was Constance de
Cezelli, a loyal supporter of Henry IV. When
that monarch, after his accession to the throne, was
struggling for supremacy with the League, the
troops of the latter, in 1590, besieged the town of
Leucates, in Languedoc. It was defended by the
Huguenots, under the command of M. de Barri,
governor of the place. The latter was captured by
means of a pretended conference; but he contrived
to write to his wife, Constance de Cezelli, bidding
her to take the command and defend the town so
long as there was any hope of success. Constance,
according to his commands, maintained order in
Leucates, and encouraged the soldiers by frequently
appearing on the walls with a pike in her hand.
When the Leaguers discovered who it was that

commanded the garrison they thought to frighten
her into a surrender by threatening to put her
husband to death if she did not give up the town.
She possessed much private property, which she
offered as ransom for her husband ; but she declared
that she could never purchase his life by an act of
treason.

M. de Barri was put to the torture, for the
besiegers thought that he would command his wife
to open the gates.   But he braved all their menaces,
and when they were compelled, soon after, to raise
the siege the governor of Leucates was strangled.

Although Constance was overwhelmed with grief
and horror, she would not allow the soldiers to avenge
the death of M. de Barri on some Roman Catholic
prisoners.

Henry IV. sent Constance de Cezelli a commission
appointing her governor of Leucates, with a reversion
in favour of her son.   She held this office for twenty-
.seven years, and proved herself thoroughly competent for the duties of governor.

On the 26th July, 1581, the United Netherlands
declared their independence, and invited the Duke
of Anjou to rule over them.   But, although the
prince entered the country with five thousand horse
and twelve thousand foot, the military genius of
Alexander Farnese, the Spanish governor, together

with the vacillating conduct of the Dutch themselves,
frustrated all his efforts, and he was compelled to
disband his forces and leave the country. The
greater number of his soldiers joined the standard of
the Prince d'Espinoy, governor of Tournai.

Alexander Farnese laid siege, on the 1st of October,
to the important city of Tournai. In the absence of
the Prince d'Espinoy, the Princess, Christine de
Lalaing, took the command, and conducted the
defence in a manner worthy of her distinguished .
relatives Count Horn and Admiral de Montmorency.
The Prince of Parma summoned Tournai to
surrender, but Christine gave him a defiant refusal,
and set so courageous an example to the soldiers
that they made a resolute defence. The princess
superintended all the defences in person, and directed
all the officers. She appeared daily on the walls,
and in one of the assaults was wounded in the arm,
though, despite this, she refused to retire till the
Spaniards had been repulsed.

After a siege of two months' duration, it became
impossible to hold the place any longer. The walls
were gradually undermined from without, and the
fidelity of the garrison was tampered with by Father
Géry, a Dominican friar. The Protestants in the city,
not knowing what moment an insurrection would
break out amongst the Catholic inhabitants, insisted
upon surrendering the place. Christine finding herself

deserted by both Protestants and Catholics, obtained honourable terms, and left the city with all the honours of war, carrying all her personal property with her.  Farnese, moreover, accepted one hundred thousand crowns in place of sacking the city.

As the princess passed through the gates she was received with an outburst of applause from the Spanish army, with whom she had acquired a high reputation through her courage.  Parma entered the city on November 30th.

In September, 1863, a statue was raised to Christine de Lalaing in the city, which, nearly three centuries before, she had so nobly defended.

In 1588 a panic flew from one end of England to the other on the threatened invasion of the Spanish Armada.  As it was supposed that the invaders would attempt to sail up the Thames, several thousand volunteers were assembled at Tilbury, under command of the Earl of Leicester.  "Vnto the sayd army," says Richard Hackluyt, "came in proper person, the Queen's most roiall Maiestie, representing Tomyris, that Scythian princesse, or rather diuine Pallas her selfe."

On the 8th of August, Queen Elizabeth, mounted on a white charger, a marshal's *bâton* grasped in her hand, rode through the camp, where she was received with enthusiastic acclamations by both volunteers

and regulars drawn up on a hill near Tilbury church.
Forbidding any of her retinue to follow her, she was
attended only by the Earls of Ormonde and Leicester; the latter bearing before her the Sword of
State. She was also followed by a page, who had the
honour of carrying her " white-plumed regal helmet."
The queen's costume was a mixture of the military
uniform and the fashionable ladies' attire of the
period. Beneath a corslet of polished steel descended
" a farthingale of such monstrous amplitude, that,"
observes Miss Strickland, " it is wonderful how
her high-mettled war-horse submitted to carry a lady
encumbered with a gabardine of so strange a fashion."

Riding bare-headed through the ranks, she
addressed the warriors in an'oration well calculated
to inspire them with enthusiasm. It concluded
amidst vociferous and long continued cheering.

After the dispersion of the Invincible Armada,
Elizabeth celebrated a triumph, in imitation of the
ancient Romans. She rode in a triumphal chariot
from her palace to St. Paul's cathedral, where the
" enseignes and colours of ye vanquished Spaniards,"
were displayed to the delighted gaze of the
citizens.

During the Border Wars between England and
Scotland women had frequent opportunities of local
distinction. Holinshed, speaking of a skirmish

which took place at Naworth, in 1570, between Lord
Hursden and Leonard Dacres, says the latter had in
his army " many desperate women, who there gave
the adventure of their lives, and fought right
stoutly."

The Duchy of Lorraine, or Lothringen, was, for
many centuries, a subject of contention between
France and Germany.  It was for a long time a fief
of the German empire ; but from the middle of the
sixteenth century, the royal family of France became
connected with its rulers, and assumed thenceforth
a right to interfere in its internal arrangements.
During the Thirty Years' War the French drove
Duke Charles from his throne, on account of his
close connection with Austria.

It was during this war that Madame St.
Balmont, who has been styled a second Joan of
Arc, performed the gallant deeds for which she
became so famous.  Barbara of Ernecourt, was
born in 1609, at the Castle of Neuville, situated
between Verdun and Bar.  She belonged to a
good family in Lorraine, and from her earliest
childhood she trained herself in military exercises
and the use of arms.  Her chief delight was hunting, and every kind of field sport, which the Abbé
Arnould remarks, " is a kind of war."  One day
when she was engaging in her favourite pastime,

she met with the Count de St. Belmont, and, being mutually charmed, they married shortly after.

Barbara was scarcely more than a girl when she married, and at this time her face was excessively pretty, though it was afterwards spoiled by the small pox—when, so far from being made unhappy by the loss of her beauty, " she was as pleased," says the Abbé Arnould, " to be marked with it as other women are afflicted on a similar occasion, and said that it would enable her to look more like a man." Her figure, however, was small and clumsily made; but she was robust, and able to bear a considerable amount of fatigue without being overcome by it.

When the French invaded Lorraine, the Count de St. Belmont, who had always occupied a high place in the estimation of the duke, now actively employed himself resisting the invaders, while Barbara remained as custodian of his castle and estates. Unfortunately, the duke's high opinion of M. de St. Belmont's military talents led the latter into a serious dilemma; for, being given the command of a fortress, he felt himself bound in honour to defend it for several days against the French. In those days there was, it would seem, a rigid code of the military law—doubtless first intro- duced through humane feelings—by which officers in charge of strongholds refusing to surrender, after all hope of success was gone, were to be punished in the most degrading manner. When this feeble stronghold was taken, the French leaders seriously debated the expediency of hanging their antagonist.

Meanwhile the countess, having been contemptuously treated by a cavalry officer who had taken up his abode on one of her husband's estates, despatched a cartel, signed "Le Chevalier de St. Belmont," purporting to be written by her husband's brother. They crossed swords, and Barbara almost immediately disarmed her opponent; then, picking up his sword and handing it to him with a gracious smile, she said:—

"You thought, sir, I make no doubt, that you were fighting with Le Chevalier de St. Belmont; it is, however Madame de St. Belmont of that name who returns you your sword, and begs you in future to pay more regard to the requests of ladies."

The officer, not caring to show his face in the vicinity, disappeared immediately and was never heard of again.

Barbara's reputation was considerably raised by this duel; several gentlemen in the neighbourhood took refuge in the village and put themselves under her orders. At their head she made frequent raids into those parts of the country occupied by the French. She was always victorious, and almost invariably brought home some trophies in arms or baggage, for, in addition to courage, she possessed great prudence and foresight.

The Peace of Westphalia, in 1648, put an end to the Thirty Years' War, and settled, for a time, the affairs of Lorraine. Barbara laid down the sword and took up the pen, which she wielded quite as skilfully. Her first work, "Les Jumeaux Martyrs," appeared in 1651; other works of equal merit followed. After the death of her husband she gave herself up entirely to religion, to which she had always been devotedly attached, and retired into a convent. She died before taking the veil, May 22nd, 1660, at the age of fifty-one.

Although there was none of that unfeminine coarseness which so often attaches to women who pass the greater part of their lives in camps, Barbara was always more at her ease in male society than in that of her own sex, in which she felt embarrassed, awkward. While her courage rendered her famous throughout France and Germany, her charity and the zeal which she displayed in the service of the poor, rendered Madame de St. Belmont respected and beloved by persons of every rank who dwelt in the neighbourhood.

Christina of Sweden, daughter of Gustavus Adol-

13—2

phus, the great Protestant hero of the Thirty Years'
War, inherited her father's native love for battles,
soldiers, even the smell of powder—all, in fact, that
pertains to a warrior's life.   When she was about
two years old, her father took her to Calmar.   The
governor did not know whether to give the customary
salute, afraid lest the child might be frightened by
the noise of the cannon.   But Gustavus, whom he
consulted, replied, after a moment's hesitation :—

"Fire !   The girl is the daughter of a soldier, and
should be accustomed to it early."

The salute was therefore given.   Christina clapped
her hands in delight.

"More !  More !" she cried.

Pleased to see her evident predilection for the
taste of gunpowder, Gustavus Adolphus took his
daughter, soon after, to see a grand review.   She
displayed even greater delight than before, and
Gustavus said, with a smile :—

"Very well; you shall go, I am resolved, where
you shall have enough of this."

However, the early death of Gustavus Adolphus
hindered him from ever fulfilling this promise; and
Christina, in her memoirs, regrets that she was not
permitted to learn the art of war under so illustrious
a master.

In 1647, at the age of twenty-nine, Christina
resigned the crown of Sweden.   Passing through

Denmark and Germany, she proceeded to Belgium; and from Innspruck she went to Rome; which she entered in state, attired in the costume of an Amazon, and mounted on a war-horse.

## IX.

### THE AMAZONS IN SOUTH AMERICA.

**D**OWN from the lofty Andes rolls the majestic Amazon, the largest river in the world. From its sources to the Atlantic the length is upwards of four thousand miles. The banks are clothed with immense impenetrable forests of pine, cedar, red-wood, holly, and cinnamon, affording a haunt to savage jaguars, bears, leopards, tigers, wild boars, and a great variety of venemous serpents; and abounding, too, in birds of the most beautiful plumage, and apes of the most fantastic appearance. The waters swarm with alligators, turtles, and almost every description of fish. The shores and islands were formerly peopled by numerous tribes of Indians, who have either become extinct or retired further up the mountains.

This majestic river was first explored in 1540–41, by Francisco Orellana, a Spanish adventurer. Gonzalo Pizarro, brother of the Marquis of Pizarro, started with Orellana from Zumaque, where they met by accident. Together they descended the river Coca in search of the wondrous El Dorado, which, they had been told, was situated on the banks of a great river into which the Coca flowed. During the voyage they met with innumerable difficulties, and suffered great hardships, especially from the want of provisions. Several of their followers fell ill; and at last Pizarro constructed a brigantine, and embarked his invalids on board, with two hundred thousand livres in gold. He gave Orellana the command, and remained behind with the rest of the adventurers; desiring Orellana, if successful, to return with supplies. The latter, having entered at last a broad river, whose shores were so distant from each other that the waters seemed like those of an inland sea, was certain he had almost reached El Dorado. On the last day of December, 1540, he resolved not to turn back; so, letting himself go with the current, he abandoned his comrades under Pizarro to their fate.

At the mouth of the Nayho, Orellana was cautioned by an old Indian chief to beware of the warlike women. At the River Canuriz, between the mouth

of the Xingu and the Rio Negro, he encountered
a hostile tribe of Indians who opposed his landing.
Blows were exchanged; several fell on each side.
Amongst the slain were several women, who had
fought quite as bravely as the men. Orellana was,
of course, the victor, and lived to carry home to
Europe an account (improved and embellished) of a
nation of Amazons who lived in South America, and
made war on the Indians.

Thenceforth a legend existed among the European
adventurers that a nation of female warriors dwelt
somewhere on the South American continent. The
river, hitherto called the Marañon, from its first
discoverer, was re-christened as the Amazons' river;
and a large tract of country, with indefinable limits,
was set down in the maps under the somewhat
vague denomination of Amazonia.

Whether the natives first told the Europeans, or
whether the latter, with a view to increase the
wonders of the New World, invented the story and
told it to the natives, none can tell; but even before
the voyage of Orellana, a tradition existed amongst
both natives and colonists that a nation of armed
women dwelt somewhere in America. Christopher
Columbus was told that the small island of Man-
danino, or Matinino (Montserrat), was inhabited
solely by female warriors.

Since the days of Orellana, there have been found

plenty of travellers to confirm the story and add
their testimony to its truth. Hernando de Ribeira,
a follower of Cabega de Vega, the Conquistador of
Paraguay, asserted in 1545 that he had been told of
a nation of Amazons who lived on the western shore
of a large lake poetically termed " The Mansion of
the Sun," because that orb sinks into its waters
every evening. Father d'Acugna, in his " Discovery
of the River Amazon," declares that the various
tribes of Indians (amongst others, the Toupinambous)
dwelling around the Amazon, assured him again and
again that a republic of female warriors did exist in
that region ; several chiefs said they themselves had
been in the country of the Amazons on a visit. If,
says d'Acugna, the tradition is not true, it is certainly
the greatest of all the fables invented about the New
World. The Indians all believed that the Amazons
possessed vast treasures, sufficient to enrich many
kingdoms ; but no one dared to attack so warlike a
nation, to whom liberty was dearer than all the
riches in the world, and who knew how to send their
poisoned shafts straight to the heart. D'Acugna
fixes the residence of the Amazons on the banks of
the Canuriz, on lofty, almost inaccessible mountains.

"When their neighbours visit them," he says,
" at a time appointed by themselves, they receive
them with bows and arrows in their hands, which

they exercise as if about to engage with enemies.
But knowing the object of their visitors, they lay
these weapons down, and welcome as their guests
the strangers, who remain with them a few days."

André Thevet, in his work "Les Singularités de la
France Antarctique," Paris, 1558, makes the arrival
of the Amazons' guests the subject of a pictorial
illustration.

In 1595, Sir Walter Raleigh, wishing to make a
fortune in a hurry, undertook an expedition to
Guiana to seek for the golden city of Manoa. Most
probably he had read Thevet's work, an English
translation of which, by Bynneman, appeared in
1568; and he made the most careful enquiries after
the Amazons. But, like his predecessors, he was
doomed to disappointment.

"I made inqvirie," says he (in his book ' The Dis-
courie of the Large, Rich, and Bewtifvl Empire of
Gviana') "amongst the most ancient and best
traueled of the *Orenoqveponi*, and I had knowledge
of all the riuers betweene *Orenoqve* and *Amazones*,
and was uery desirovs to vnderstand the trvth of the
warlike women, bicavce of some it is beleeved, of
others not; though I digresse from my pvrpose, yet
I will set doune what hath been deliuered to me for
troth of those women, and I spake with a *Casiqve*, or
lord of the people, that told me he had been in the
riuer, and beyond it also, the nations of those women

are on the sovth side of the riuer in a prouince of *Topago,* and their chiefest strength and retraicts are in the Islands scitvate on the sovth side of the entrance, some sixty leagves within the movth of the said riuer."

After entering into some details about the reception of their guests in the month of April, when, he says, "this one moneth they feast, davnce, and drinke," he gives an account of the treatment of children, which bears a suspicious resemblance to the stories related of the ancient Amazons. He further tells us the South American Amazons were "said to be very crvell and bloodthirsty, especially to svch as offer to inuade their territories."

In 1599 an abridged Latin translation of Raleigh's work appeared at Nuremberg, at the cost of Levinus Hulsius, geographer and collector. It was illustrated by five coloured plates; the third representing the joyful reception of the Amazons' visitors, and their subsequent amusements; the fourth showing the treatment bestowed on prisoners of war, who are seen hung up by the heels to trees, where they serve as targets for the skill of their captors, while their ultimate fate is hinted by the figures of several Amazons preparing huge fires.

At the close of the seventeenth century, Father Cyprian Baraza, a Jesuit missionary who went among the South American Indians, gave an ac-

count of some Amazonian tribes who dwelt to the west
of the Paraquay, in 12° south latitude. M. de Con-
damine, who read a " Relation abrégée d'un Voyage,"
etc., before the Académie des Sciences in 1745,
brought forward several testimonies to the existence
of the Amazons, whom he described as a society of
independent women, who were visited by the sterner
sex during the month of April only. Amongst other
authorities he mentions Don Francisco Diego
Portales, and Don Francisco Torralva, two Spanish
governors of Venezuela, who agreed in declaring that
a tribe of female warriors lived in the interior of
Guiana.

Thirty years later he was supported by a Portuguese astronomer, Don Ribeiro de Sampeio
(" Diario da Viegem, no anno de 1774 et 1775 ")
who, however, spoke only by hearsay. Gili, the
missionary, was told by an Indian of the Quaqua
tribe that the Aikeambenanos ("women living
alone ") dwelt on the banks of the Cuchinero, which
falls into the Orinoco opposite the island of Taran,
between Cayeara and Alta Gracia.

Count Pagan, in his " Relation de la Rivière des
Amazones," after testifying to the existence of the
nation, observes, in his florid style " Que l'Asie ne
se vante plus de ses comptes véritables ou fabuleuses
des Amazones. L'Amérique ne lui céde point cet
avantage. . . . . Et que le fleuve de Thermodoon ne

soit plus enflé de la gloire de ces conquérantes les guerrières."

The Abbé Guyon, in his " Histoire des Amazons," Paris, 1740, expresses great faith in the story of these South American dames; and suggests that they were colonised by the African Amazons, who might, he suggests, have passed from the Old to the New World by the now submerged isle of Atlantis. But his testimony is of little value, as it evidently rests almost entirely upon D'Acugna's report.

Even within the last twenty or thirty years, many Indian tribes have expressed their belief in the existence of the Amazons. Those who dwell on the Essequibo, the Rupunni, and the lower Corentyn, gravely assured Sir Robert Schomburgh, in 1844, that separate tribes of women still lived on the upper part of the Corentyn, in a country called Marawonne; and the narrators went so much into detail that Sir Robert and his companions were almost inclined to believe them. The natives further told them that when they had journeyed some distance above the great cataracts of the Corentyn, at a point where two gigantic rocks (named by the Indians Pioomoco and Surama) rose from either shore, they would be in the country of the Woruisamocos, or Amazons.

Sir Robert, while travelling over the vast savannahs, frequently came upon heaps of broken pottery, which the Macusion Indians said were relics of the

Woruisamocos, who had formerly dwelt there. The Caribs were especially persistent in declaring that an Amazonian republic still existed in the centre of Guiana "in those districts which no European had ever visited."

The explorers of the river Amazon were formerly stopped by the great cataracts on the Rio Trombetas, and in many instances they were murdered by ferocious Indians who inhabit the upper branches. Naturally those parts of the river which remained unexplored were supposed to be the land of the "bellicose dames." In 1842-44 M. Montravel, commander of the French war-ship "La Boulonnaise," surveyed the Amazon from the sea as high up as the Rio Negro, and heard the same tale in the region of the Rio Trombetas. Thus, from the west as well as from the north, Europeans heard of a nation of Amazons dwelling in the central districts of Guiana.

Humboldt believed to a certain extent in the tradition. His idea was that women, in various parts of South America, have now and then wearied of the degrading condition in which they are held, and occasionally united themselves into bands, as fugitive negroes sometimes do, and that the necessity of preserving their independence has made them warriors.

Southey, in his "History of Brazil," makes a very

trite observation concerning the female warriors of the New World. "Had we never," says he, "heard of the Amazons of antiquity, I should, without hesitation, believe in those of America. Their existence is not the less likely for this reason, and yet it must be admitted that the probable truth is made to appear suspicious by its resemblance to a known fable."

## X.

" THERE are three sorts of things in the world," says the Abbé Brotier, "that know no kind of restraint, and are governed by passion and brutality— family quarrels, religious disputes, and civil wars." The truth of these words is undeniable, more especially as the last is very frequently brought about by its forerunners. The war between Charles I. and the Parliament was prosecuted on both sides with so much bitterness, that, in certain instances, the conduct of the officers and generals savoured more of private feud than public zeal.

The Irish Rebellion of 1641 was one of many unfortunate occurrences which precipitated the revolution at home, for not only did the Republican party take advantage of the King's difficulties to increase its own power, but the Irish rebels envenomed the bitterness between King and Commons by declaring that they were empowered, by Royal Commission, to defend his Majesty's prerogatives against a Puritanical, levelling Government.

The Irish rebels stormed many a castle belonging to English nobles or gentry. Amongst others, they beleaguered, in April, 1642, the Castle of Geashill, in King's County, the residence of Lettice Digby, Baroness of Offaley. This lady, though upwards of sixty years old, and a widow, retained all the fire and energy of youth. She closed the gates, and made a most resolute defence, refusing to hear any proposal for surrender, for the castle, being defended on all sides by bogs and woods, was very difficult of access. She was at last relieved by the approach of Viscount Lisle and Sir Charles Coote with one hundred and twenty foot and three hundred horse. The castle having been provisioned and supplied with ammunition, Lady Offaley chose to remain there for a time; but being again menaced by the rebels, she was relieved by Sir Richard Grenville, in October of the same year, when she retired to her

mansion at Coles Hill, in Warwickshire, where she
died, December the 1st, 1658.

On the 25th of August, 1642, King Charles raised
his standard at Nottingham. He was at once joined
by thousands of Cavaliers; amongst others, by the
Earl of Arundell, one of his most staunch adherents.
The latter made himself so troublesome to the
Parliament that they determined to seize Wardour
Castle, his mansion. In 1643, they sent orders to
Sir Edward Hungerford, commander-in-chief of their
forces in Wiltshire, to accomplish this design. He
arrived before the castle on the 2nd of May, and as
Lord Arundell was absent, the Puritans expected
an easy conquest. But Lady Blanche, who had
been left in charge, was well supplied with provisions and ammunition: and although the garrison
consisted of barely twenty-five fighting men, she
resolved to make a brave defence.

Sir Edward Hungerford, on the arrival of Colonel
Strode with reinforcements, summoned the castle to
surrender, pretending that it contained men and
arms, money, and plate which he was ordered, by a
warrant from Parliament, to seize. Lady Arundell
declined to comply with his demands. Sir Edward
immediately ordered up his heavy guns, and commenced a bombardment which lasted from Wednes-
day the 3rd to the following Monday. The besiegers,

moreover, ran two mines under the walls, and so terrific was the explosion that the fortress was shaken to its foundations.

During the siege, Sir Edward offered again and again to grant quarter to the ladies and children if the castle would surrender ; but Lady Arundell and the other ladies rejected the proposal with disdain. The latter, too, together with the women-servants, aided in the defence in various ways; they loaded the muskets, and carried round refreshments to their gallant defenders.

According as the garrison, exhausted by the continued struggle, relaxed in its efforts, the Parliamentary soldiers redoubled their attacks. They applied petards to the garden-door, they flung balls of wild-fire through the dismantled windows, causing much damage to the apartments in the castle, destroying valuable pictures, rich carvings, statuettes, costly vases, chairs and couches, mirrors, and various works of almost priceless worth.

After the siege had lasted nine days, Lady Arundell, finding the castle was no longer tenable, demanded a parley. Articles of surrender were drawn up, by which it was stipulated, firstly, that the garrison and all the inmates of the castle should be granted quarter ; secondly, that the ladies and servants should have all their wearing apparel, and that sixty serving-men, chosen by the ladies them-

14—2

selves, should be permitted to attend them wherever they might please to retire; thirdly, that the furniture of the castle was to be saved from plunder or destruction.

The Puritans violated, without scruple, the treaty, destroyed or mutilated everything of value in the castle, and left with the inmates nothing but the clothes they wore. Lady Arundell, with the women and children, was carried prisoner to Shaftesbury. Thither, too, five van-loads of costly furniture were borne in triumph as the spoils of the vanquished.

The loss to Lord Arundell by the devastation and plunder of Wardour Castle was estimated at one hundred thousand pounds.

The Parliament, thinking their prisoners were insecure at Shaftesbury, wished to remove them to Bath. But the town was infected with small-pox and plague; and Lady Arundell refused so stubbornly to consent, that her captors left her where she was, but took her children to Dorchester.

Lady Arundell survived the siege only five years; and at her death, she was buried, with her husband, in the chapel of Wardour Castle.

In point of heroic valour, Lady Arundell was outdone by Lady Mary Bankes, wife of Sir John Bankes, Lord Chief Justice of the Common Pleas. In August, 1643, Parliament despatched Sir William

Earle with a strong force to reduce Corfe Castle, the
family residence of Sir John, in the Isle of Purbeck.
Thinking to gain possession by stratagem, Sir
William sent a party of forty sailors to demand four
field-pieces which were in the castle. Lady Bankes,
suspecting their real object, went to the gate, and
requested the sailors to show their warrant. They
produced one, signed by several Parliamentary Com-
missioners. Thereupon Lady Bankes retired into the
castle ; and although there were only five men within
the walls, they mounted the field-pieces with the
assistance of the female servants, and having loaded
one of them, fired it off, and drove the sailors away.

Sir William Earle now tried to starve the castle
into a surrender. Lady Bankes affected a wish to
treat for the surrender of the guns; but her real
object was, that the besiegers, relaxing in their
careful blockade, would give greater facilities for
introducing fresh supplies to the garrison. The
event justified her hopes. She also obtained the
help of Captain Lawrence, commanding a company
of Royalists.

The Puritans, about six hundred in number,
assaulted the castle, and endeavoured to carry it by
a *coup de main.* But the brave little garrison, sallying forth, drove away the besiegers and brought
back nine oxen. Again the besiegers tried to
take the castle by storm. Dividing their forces,

one party attacked the middle ward, which was defended by Captain Lawrence and his company, while the other division assaulted the upper ward, held by Lady Bankes with her daughters, her female servants, and five soldiers, who hurled down huge stones and red-hot coals on the heads of the storming party. At last, after losing one hundred men in the assault, the Parliamentary forces retreated from before Corfe Castle. The blockade had lasted, altogether, six weeks.

Lady Bankes lived to see the Restoration, and died in April, 1661. She was interred in the south aisle of Rislipp church. The following inscription was placed upon her monument by her eldest son :—

"To the memory of

"The Lady Mary Bankes, the only daughter of Rafe Hawtrey, of Rislipp, in the County of Middlesex, Esquire, the wife and widow of the Honourable Sir John Bankes, Knight, late Lord Chief Justice of his late Majesty's Court of Common Pleas, and of the Privy Council to his late Majesty King Charles the First, of blessed memory; who, having had the honour to have borne, with a constancy and courage above her sex, a noble proportion of the late calamity, and the happiness to have outlived them so far as to have seen the restitution of the government, with great peace of mind laid down her most desired life the 19th day of April, 1661. Sir Ralphe Bankes,

her son and heir, hath dedicated this. She left four
sonnes—first, Sir Ralphe; second, Jerome; third,
Charles; fourth, William (since dead, without issue);
and six daughters."

The Earl of Derby was one of the most prominent
Cavalier leaders. In 1643, while awaiting a siege at
Lathom House, Lancashire, his family mansion, the
earl received intelligence that Parliament had despatched troops to annex his miniature kingdom, the
Isle of Man. Wishing to preserve the island as a final
retreat for his royal master, in case of misfortune
overtaking him, he left Lathom House in charge of
Charlotte, his countess, and set off to the Isle of Man.

On the 27th of May, 1643, Mr. Holland, governor
of Manchester, despatched a messenger to Lathom,
commanding Lady Derby either to subscribe to the
propositions of Parliament or surrender the mansion.
She refused compliance with either alternative; and
for nearly a year contrived, though closely blockaded,
to keep the enemy from coming to open hostilities.
At last, on the 24th of February, 1644, Parliament
despatched three colonels to Lathom House. Before
their arrival, the countess hastened to lay in provisions and ammunition, and to arm a sufficient
number of retainers to serve as a garrison.

The countess determined not to surrender on any
terms, and rejected every proposal. "Though a

woman," said she, "and a stranger divorced from
her friends and robbed of her estates, she was ready
to receive their utmost violence, trusting in GOD for
protection and deliverance."

Hostilities having commenced, the Parliamentary
army pushed the siege with great vigour. The
countess conducted the defence in person; but,
though she took the office of commander, she was
not unmindful of the spiritual welfare of her people.
She was present four times a day at public prayer,
attended by her little daughters, Catherine and Mary.

A few days after the opening of the siege, Sir
Thomas Fairfax, the Parliamentary general, received
a letter from the Earl of Derby, in which the latter,
dreading the extremes to which his wife and children
might be reduced, requested for them a free pass
through the camp of the besiegers. When this was
communicated to the countess, she thanked Sir
Thomas for his courtesy in forwarding the missive;
but replied that "she would willingly submit to her
lord's commands, and therefore willed the general to
treat with her; but till she was assured that such
was his lordship's pleasure, she would neither yield
up the house nor desert it herself, but wait for the
event according to the will of GOD."

She forwarded a similar message to her husband
at Chester.

On the 25th of April, Colonel Rigby despatched a

peremptory message, demanding the surrender of
Lathom House immediately. The countess refused:
and the siege was prosecuted with renewed vigour;
while the garrison, animated by the presence of
Lady Derby, continued to defend the house with
unabated courage. At last, on the 23rd of May,
they learnt, to their inexpressible relief, that Prince
Rupert and the Earl of Derby were in Cheshire,
marching to their aid.

When the Puritans heard of the approach of
Prince Rupert, they retreated to Bolton. On the
29th, Prince Rupert " not only relieved, but revenged
the most noble lady, his cousin," leaving one thousand
five hundred of the besiegers dead on the field, and
taking seven hundred prisoners. The next day he
presented the countess with twenty-two of those
standards which, three days previously, had been
proudly waving before Lathom House.

The countess and her children accompanied the
earl to the Isle of Man, leaving the mansion in
charge of Colonel Rawstone. The latter defended
it till the following December, when the decline of
the Royal cause obliged him to open negotiations
with Fairfax. Before they were brought to a satis-
factory conclusion, the house was treacherously
surrendered by an Irish soldier.

The earl and countess, in the midst of their
devoted adherents in the Isle of Man, defied the

threats of Parliament.   The earl was one of the
first to join the standard of Charles II. in 1651.
Captured on the borders of Cheshire, he was carried
to his own town of Bolton-le-Moors, where he was
beheaded, October 15th.  Misfortune never comes un-
accompanied.  The bereaved countess was betrayed,
with her children, by a false friend, and thrown into
prison.  She regained her liberty at the Restoration ;
and for the rest of her life dwelt, with her remaining children, at Knowsley, near Lathom, where she
died in 1663.

Although the Turks were expelled from Hungary
in the sixteenth century, they by no means gave up
their ambitious designs on that country.   Taking
advantage of the cruelty and oppression exercised
by Austria towards the Hungarians, they secretly
stirred up the nobles to revolt against their harsh
masters.  In 1678, an able leader was found in
Emeric Tekeli, or Tokolyi, who, weary of vainly
soliciting the Emperor Leopold to restore his paternal estates, resolved to take them for himself,
together with the crown of Hungary.  Setting up
his standard in Transylvania, he was soon joined by
thousands of malcontents.  Day by day the revolt
gathered strength ;  and had not the Emperor resorted to the arts of cunning and bribery, it is
probable the rebellion would have terminated in a
revolution.

Tekeli was husband of Helena, widow of Francis Ragotsky (who died in 1667), and daughter of Peter, Count Zrinyi, Ban of Croatia, who, with others, lost his head in 1671 for conspiring against Leopold. Helena was as brave as she was beautiful. By her first husband she had two sons, of whom the eldest, Francis, afterwards took a conspicuous part in the affairs of Hungary.

Tekeli commenced the war in 1678, and in 1682 he entered Buda in triumph, where he was inaugurated Prince of Upper Hungary by the nobles and the Turkish Bashaw. In the following year, the Turks, following up these successes, advanced to Vienna, which would have fallen, but for John Sobiesky and his Poles. Leopold took care to foment the growing jealousies between Tekeli and the Turks; and on the failure of the Hungarian leader in an attack on Cassau, the Bashaw of Great Waradin sent the hero in chains to Constantinople. He was released the following year; but during his imprisonment the Turks were driven from Hungary and the rebellion crushed. Helena continued to defend the rock-fortress of Mongatz (or Munkacs) with great courage for two years after the arrest of her husband; but in 1688 she was overpowered by superior numbers, and reduced to capitulate and throw herself with her sons under the protection of the Emperor.

Helena was thrown into a convent, while her
children were educated under the auspices of Leopold.
After a time she was exchanged for an Austrian
general, and permitted to join her husband in
Turkey. The Sultan, Mustapha, conferred upon
Tekeli, Widdin, and some other districts, as a sort
of feudal sovereignty; but he was afterwards
neglected by the Turkish government, and compelled
to start as a vintner in Constantinople, where he
died in 1705, in his fiftieth year. Helena, after
sharing the misfortunes and vicissitudes of his life,
died two years before him, in 1703.

A somewhat ludicrous affair happened at the
coronation of William and Mary, April 23rd, 1689.
The champion of England, according to custom,
entered Westminster Hall, and throwing down his
mailed glove, gave the customary challenge to any
one who should dare to dispute their Majesty's claim
to the crown. An old woman came in on crutches
(which she left behind her), snatched up the gauntlet,
laid her own glove in its place, and made off as fast
as she could, before any one was able to stop her.
In the glove was found a challenge for the champion
to meet her the following day in Hyde Park. This
matter occasioned much merriment at the lower end
of the hall.

Next day an old woman, similarly dressed, was

seen waiting at the appointed ground, and was con-
jectured by those who saw her, to be a soldier in
disguise. The champion, however, wisely declining
any warlike contest with one of the fair sex, refused
to keep the appointment.

Madlle. de la Tour du Pin Gouvernail, better
known as Madlle. de la Charce, heroine of the war
between Louis Quatorze and the Duke of Savoy,
was the daughter of Pierre de la Tour du Pin,
Marquis de la Charce, lieutenant-general of the
king's armies. In 1692 the Piedmontese invaded
Dauphiné. Madlle. de la Charce, arming the
villagers on her estates, placed herself at their head,
and harassed the enemy in the mountains; her
mother, meanwhile, addressed the people in the
plains, exhorting them to remain faithful. The
sister of Madlle. de la Charce caused the cables of
the enemy's vessels to be cut. This brave family
contributed so greatly towards driving the Duke of
Savoy from Dauphiné, that Louis XIV. granted
Philis a pension, the same as he would have given to
a brave general, and allowed her to place her sword
and armour in the treasury of St. Denis.

Madlle. de la Charce was fond of literature, and
composed some very pretty verses. An anonymous
work appeared in 1731, under the title of " Mémoires

de Madlle. de la Charce." This little romance, says Langlet-Dufresnoy, is well written, and contains many historical anecdotes connected with the reign of the Grand-Monarque.

END OF VOL. I.

PRINTED BY TAYLOR AND CO.
10 LITTLE QUEEN STREET, LINCOLN'S INN FIELDS.

# Trieste

Trieste Publishing has a massive catalogue of classic book titles. Our aim is to provide readers with the highest quality reproductions of fiction and non-fiction literature that has stood the test of time. The many thousands of books in our collection have been sourced from libraries and private collections around the world.

The titles that Trieste Publishing has chosen to be part of the collection have been scanned to simulate the original. Our readers see the books the same way that their first readers did decades or a hundred or more years ago. Books from that period are often spoiled by imperfections that did not exist in the original. Imperfections could be in the form of blurred text, photographs, or missing pages. It is highly unlikely that this would occur with one of our books. Our extensive quality control ensures that the readers of Trieste Publishing's books will be delighted with their purchase. Our staff has thoroughly reviewed every page of all the books in the collection, repairing, or if necessary, rejecting titles that are not of the highest quality. This process ensures that the reader of one of Trieste Publishing's titles receives a volume that faithfully reproduces the original, and to the maximum degree possible, gives them the experience of owning the original work.

We pride ourselves on not only creating a pathway to an extensive reservoir of books of the finest quality, but also providing value to every one of our readers. Generally, Trieste books are purchased singly - on demand, however they may also be purchased in bulk. Readers interested in bulk purchases are invited to contact us directly to enquire about our tailored bulk rates. Email: customerservice@triestepublishing.com

# You May Also Like

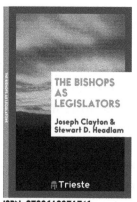

ISBN: 9780649074716
Paperback: 140 pages
Dimensions: 6.14 x 0.30 x 9.21 inches
Language: eng

# The Bishops as Legislators

## Joseph Clayton & Stewart D. Headlam

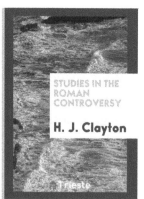

ISBN: 9780649715473
Paperback: 166 pages
Dimensions: 5.83 x 0.35 x 8.27 inches
Language: eng

# Studies in the Roman Controversy

## H. J. Clayton

www.triestepublishing.com